A+ Education

A+ Education

Choosing the Best School Option for Your Child

William Eckenwiler

Baker Books

A Division of Baker Book House Co
Grand Rapids, Michigan 49516

Published by Baker Books
a division of Baker Book House Company
P.O. Box 6287, Grand Rapids, MI 49516-6287

Printed in the United States of America

Library of Congress Cataloging-in-Publication Data is on file at the Library of Congress, Washington D.C.

ISBN 0-8010-6409-0

For current information about all releases from Baker Book House, visit our web site:

http://www.bakerbooks.com

To the nearly 12 million single parents in America,
whose educational choices are often limited
by circumstance but whose legacy belongs to us all

Contents

Acknowledgments

This book is really the product of God's shaping and transforming grace, often delivered at the hands of people he has brought into my life. I simply must offer a humble word of thanks to those so used by the Lord.

Thank you, Richard Pratt, John Scott, Rick Medlin, and Greg Ward—special men willing to look me in the eye and ask after the state of my soul.

I owe a debt of gratitude to my Lake Sumter cohort of University of Central Florida students, who breathed fresh life into my love of teaching. A special word of thanks is extended to Shellane Clark for anchoring me anew in the things that matter.

To my students, colleagues, and the board at Reformed Theological Seminary, thank you for the sabbatical and many personal expressions of support in the completion of this book. I am especially grateful to Steve Brown, John Frame, and John Muether for their willingness to lend their unique expertise to the advancement of this project.

Finally, I extend sincere gratitude to Chad Allen, my editor at Baker Books, for his skill and good humor.

Introduction

Never before in the history of America have there been so many educational choices available to parents. We have charter schools, magnet schools, and voucher systems being tried in different parts of the country. Even without the choice that vouchers provide, parents are often given a menu of public schools in their geographical area from which to choose. Businesses and philanthropists are spending private money to create public school initiatives that add to the menu of choices parents now face.

At the same time there is a wide variety of private schools, both religious and nonsectarian. In the mid-1990s nearly one in four of America's school children attended a private school. During this period Chicago recorded some 387 private schools compared to 550 public schools.[1]

Another option is home schooling, which has moved from being perceived as a highly questionable choice that parents often practiced in secret to an increasingly mainstream phenomenon. Even within the home schooling option there are many variations from which to choose.

With so many educational choices, parents often find themselves pulled in conflicting directions. Advocates of one choice or another can be rather insistent, if not militant, in their rhetoric. A colleague at work insists that public schools are beyond hope, while a neighbor talks about how her child has flourished at the local elementary school. Friends at church insist that home schooling is the only hope any of us have for our children, while a family member lobbies hard for the Christian school where he serves as principal. What's a parent to do?

With so many insistent voices advocating one educational direction over another, parents often lose perspective, not even realizing that previous generations have wrestled with similar issues. For example, in the 1950s we witnessed the publication of Rudolf Flesch's book, *Why Johnny Can't Read*, which sounded the alarm of failed public schools. Racial integration of our schools in the 1960s increased our nation's awareness of the haves and have-nots in our schools. The early 1980s brought us the explosive governmental report, *A Nation at Risk*, which once again sounded the alarm of failure and provoked decades of educational initiatives. Today, political candidates almost always have to promise some sort of educational reform to have a chance at election.

In the middle of all this, parents have struggled to make decisions about the best way to educate their children. Rich and poor, married and single, Republican and Democrat and apolitical, African American and Asian American and Caucasian, Christian and Jew and Muslim and agnostic, parents are trying to sort through the rhetoric that comes at them from every direction.

Over the last thirty years I have counseled many of these parents as they have wrestled with the issues surrounding their particular schooling concerns. What you will read in the following pages is my counsel to any who are trying to decide between public schools, private/Christian* schools, or home schooling. Before you settle in to chapter 1, however, I would like to offer more information about my perspective.

As you will read later in the book, I am a product of America's public schools, as are my two daughters. After receiving an undergraduate degree in education, I taught in public schools for nearly ten years. After leaving the classroom as a teacher, I reentered as a student, doing master's degree work at a conservative evangelical seminary, and then as a doctoral student at a state university. While completing my doctoral dissertation on home schooling, I was supervising student teachers in the local public school system, while at the same time teaching education classes at both a seminary and a local university. I continue to teach in both settings.

The Christian circles I move in are thought to be quite conservative, and many within this community have deep convictions about the virtues of home schooling or Christian schools. However, even within this community there is uncertainty and differences of opinion. When I confer with these parents of particularly strong philosophical convictions, it is not uncommon for them to admit that the decision about where to educate their child is more complicated than some would like to make it.

While at times it seems like there is a growing "movement" away from public schools, it is estimated that 90 percent of Christian parents still send their children to public schools. Some send their children to public schools by choice and others feel as if they have no choice, but the fact is the vast majority of Christian children are in public schools.

*When I use the term "private/Christian," I am referring to private schools that are either Christian or non-Christian.

The decision about which educational option to choose is a complicated process that nags millions of parents. This book assumes that whether we are talking about Christians, Jews, Muslims, or any other particular group, within these groups there are informed and loving parents who choose to send their children to public schools. Moreover, this book assumes there are equally informed and loving parents in these same groups who opt for private schooling or home schooling. Further, these same parents may change their minds along the way, perhaps several times, for all sorts of reasons. This book is not, therefore, an attempt to convince you that one choice is better than another. Instead, I want to be of service by providing you with information that will help you make the best decision for your particular situation.

If you told me that you had studied the matter, consulted with a number of friends and experts, and had decided to enroll your children in public schools, I would say, "God bless you. I will stand with you in that decision. However, having made that choice, may I tell you some things you should probably know as you begin this journey? I'm not necessarily trying to change your mind. I simply want to help you do the best parenting job possible given this particular decision." I would say the same thing to the home schooling parent and the parent who chose private schools. What I would then tell you is the message of this book.

Chapter 1 offers a foundational message of responsibility and hope to parents, urging them to embrace the great privilege that is theirs in the raising of their children. Chapter 2 introduces us to some of the current concerns over discipline and safety in the public schools that have many wondering if they should consider an alternative to public schools. Public school concerns of a more academic nature are addressed in chapter 3, while chapter 4 explores some very important but almost invisible lessons we almost never talk about when discussing educational concerns.

Chapter 5 is a message of hope to parents in the face of the concerns raised in the previous chapters, reporting the positive effects of parental involvement. Before leaving the discussion of public schools and moving on to the options of home schooling or private/Christian schooling, chapter 6 provides an important historical overview of schooling choices in America. Chapter 7 gives consideration to the strengths and weaknesses of the private/Christian school option, while chapter 8 offers a similar treatment of home schooling. Chapter 9 concludes with some summary thoughts on all three education options as well as words of encouragement for every parent wrestling with school choice.

Because this book includes a critique of three major educational choices, there is some negative ground to cover. That is the nature of critique and warning. Nevertheless, I have tried to give voice to this critique from inside the various educational camps. In other words, when I examine the public schools I will be referring to research and people that either work within that system or have some level of commitment to the public school effort. The voices will shift as I move to the other educational choices, and you will hear from those within each educational community. I have done this in an attempt to avoid launching missiles of criticism from one group into the camp of another. While I may not have been entirely successful, my goal has been to ratchet down the militant rhetoric of advocacy, while at the same time giving parents real insight into the consequences of their choice.

As you sort through issues raised in the following pages, I hope you will hear one predominating message. That message is an invitation to embrace the sobering privilege of parental responsibility whatever your educational choice might be. I believe parental involvement is crucial to the success or failure of any educational option and is the safest way to ensure that your children receive the best education possible.

Who's in Charge Here?

When it comes to school choice, sorting through the issues can be confusing and frustrating. People can be militant and dogmatic about their school-choice convictions, and the voices are sometimes shrill. Well-meaning friends and family increase the difficulty of your decision as you feel the pressure to avoid disagreement with those you value.

Because sorting through all the issues and opinions can be tough, I want to begin our discussion in a way that may surprise you. Instead of starting with an examination of educational choices and their relative merits, I invite you to consider something more basic. A foundational understanding of authority, obedience, and parental responsibility will ultimately make your educational decision easier. Let me explain. Consider the following three scenarios.

Have you ever observed a mother scolding her young child of two or three? Imagine yourself as that toddler; your hand gets slapped or your diaper gets swatted or a time-out is threatened. Tears and resistance and various forms of reconciliation play out in familiar patterns throughout the day as your mother or father works hard at shaping your behavior.

Our second scenario involves an older youngster. You are now around the age of ten, asking permission to spend the night at a friend's house. With permission denied you resort to whining and demanding an explanation for what seems to be an arbitrary bit of injustice. You are well beyond diapers at this point, but the patterns of resistance and various degrees of reconciliation are familiar. After a series of intentionally vague explanations, your mother finally explains that she does not feel comfortable with your friend's family and the way they conduct themselves. Maybe she is leery of too much television or nonchaperoned access to the Internet or a laissez-faire approach to discipline or bedtimes. This was likely exasperating to you, but your parents' decision was based on a desire to control your exposure to an unhealthy environment.

In our third scenario you are even older. Perhaps you remember when as a teenager you were forbidden to ride in cars driven by certain friends of yours. Maybe you remember what you thought were unreasonable curfews or dress codes. Rules seemed to be everywhere, controlling you unrelentingly. There were rules about dating prior to a certain age, use of lipstick, getting ears pierced, homework, telephone use, and a whole host of money-related issues. This business of authority and obedience begins early and nips at our heels all the days of our lives.

We balk at authority from the earliest age. Years ago I was in a Sunday school class in which the teacher asked the group what we thought would be a good definition of Christian maturity regarding this matter of authority and obedience. An elderly woman chose a simple four-word answer, "Broken to the bit." Her definition conjures up images of a wild stallion, almost crazed by attempts to place a saddle on its back or a bit in its mouth. It's easy for me to recognize the wild and frantic part of me that resists authority. Like all of us, I have an innate desire to buck authority from my back and trample it under my hooves. With natural inclinations like these, it is not surprising that much of Scripture speaks to matters of obedience and authority.

Whether it is a question of children obeying parents or citizenry submitting to government, God admonishes us to learn proper submission to authority structures that he has designed according to his infinite wisdom. When we say God is Lord, we are saying among other things that he has authority over us; he has a right to expect obedience. When he commands, "Let there be light," there is light. When he commands, "Do not kill," we should not kill.

The Lord of all authority often delegates portions of his authority to human beings—parents, teachers, judges, kings. Just as he says "obey me," he also says, "Children, obey your parents in the Lord" (Ephesians 6:1). Of course, God's authority is unlimited, while the authority of human beings is limited. Even though God gives authority over children primarily to parents, parents are not at liberty to command their children to do anything they want them to do. God tells fathers not to exasperate their children. This is the great burden of every parent who cares—to raise and nurture their children in the most responsible manner, always with an eye on both the character and mandates of God.

Even though human authority is limited by God, it is still genuine authority. We are called by God to learn obedience to parents, the speed limit, the IRS auditor, teachers, our Little League coach, employers, flight attendants, and anyone else in legitimate authority. Obedience to legitimate authority is, in effect, obedience to God himself. Conversely, disobedience to legitimate authority is best understood as a clenched fist raised against God.

While we might be ready to concede that everyone must learn to submit to proper authority, there is an equally important burden that rests upon those who are in authority. The Bible rightly directs those in authority to exercise it in a way that does not exasperate, discourage, or exploit those who are called to submit. People who exercise authority certainly should follow these biblical mandates, but often there is a more basic problem: they fail to exercise their authority at all.

Can you imagine a policeman standing by and watching a convenience store being robbed, or a basketball referee never blowing his whistle over an obvious infraction? How about a parent who allows his child to eat a supper of bubblegum and cookies?

As ridiculous as these scenarios sound, only slightly less startling are parents who drop their children off at a playmate's house without knowing anything about the environment in which the child will spend the next four hours. I'm not referring to the possibility of child abuse, to which we all must be increasingly more vigilant. I'm referring to the value system that will be lived out before the child's eyes in the playmate's home. Possible concerns include what the child will be exposed to in terms of manners, language, cleanliness, use of humor, honesty, discipline, and safety, not to mention whether or how closely the children's activities will be monitored.

The issues will vary from situation to situation, and it is impossible to establish a set of specific criteria that would render a given situation acceptable to every parent. My challenge is for parents to do their best to be aware of the influences affecting their children, and then to lead on the basis of that awareness.

I suspect most people would agree that many parents have shirked their responsibility to take charge of the development of their children. Divorce rates are up, truancy is up, guns are in schools, teens get pregnant, and so on. We all know how bad it is; what I want to do is gently yet firmly challenge you to consider whether you yourself have let go of this responsibility. To do this, let's look at how Scripture views children.

Psalm 127:3–5 states,

> Sons are a heritage from the LORD,
>   children a reward from him.
> Like arrows in the hands of a warrior
>   are sons born in one's youth.
> Blessed is the man
>   whose quiver is full of them.

This passage, along with many others, lets us know that children are a gift from God himself! They come to us as a sacred trust, but unlike an inanimate object, children are living organisms subject to the continuous stream of everyday influences brought about by people and events. Part of the duty that comes with receiving the gift of children is careful attention to influences that shape their values and beliefs about God, people, and how the world is to be understood. Jesus himself saved some of his strongest language for those who would lead children astray:

> At that time the disciples came to Jesus and asked, "Who is the greatest in the kingdom of heaven?"
>
> He called a little child and had him stand among them. And he said: "I tell you the truth, unless you change and become like little children, you will never enter the kingdom of heaven. Therefore, whoever humbles himself like this child is the greatest in the kingdom of heaven.
>
> And whoever welcomes a little child like this in my name welcomes me. But if anyone causes one of these little ones who believe in me to sin, it would be better

21

for him to have a large millstone hung around his neck and to be drowned in the depths of the sea.

Matthew 18:1–6

Children are to be understood as a very special, even sacred gift from God. Additionally, Scripture tells us proper development of children is an issue dear to the heart of God. As parents, we bear the ultimate responsibility for our children's growth. God did not give our children to the State, a school, another set of parents in the neighborhood, a nursery worker, a local church, or even a grandparent. Any of these may be a significant part of your child's life, but the ultimate responsibility never ceases to belong to you, the parent.

If we can embrace this core concept of ultimate parental responsibility, we will know better how to approach all those other people and situations that typically become a part of the fabric of a child's life.

My challenge for parents to assume ultimate responsibility for their children is not meant to drive parents neurotically to hide their children from the world. Realistically, we place our children under the supervision of a variety of people, from babysitters to family members to teachers, dentists, scout leaders, piano instructors, and so on. But even as we voluntarily place our children in the care of various people, we are the ones deciding the who, what, when, where, and why of each and every encounter. Implicit in each decision is the responsibility to evaluate how healthy each situation is. This concept is so important that our legal system makes provision for it.

Promising not to get too technical, let me introduce you to a Latin phrase that our government uses, *in loco parentis*. Simply put, *in loco parentis* means "in the place of parents." Recognizing the vulnerability of children, the State provides that someone must accept legal responsibility for a child at all times. Thus, if a child is injured due to negligence, the State will have the right to hold a particular person or group of persons responsible. If parents, for example, hand their child over in good faith to a piano teacher, they assume the piano teacher will behave responsibly *in loco parentis*. Where negligence is proven on the part of the piano teacher, the State will hold that person accountable.

I should point out that *in loco parentis* is not a license given to caregivers to do whatever they like with the child. In fact, much discussion and litigation surrounding this concept of *in loco parentis* is centered around the extent of responsibility and authority.

A schoolteacher paddles a student or requires the student to write "I must not talk in class" five hundred times. A parent takes issue, claiming the teacher had no right to require a particular punishment. A college freshman is paralyzed in a car accident on campus. Alcohol is involved. The parents of the student sue the college for not exercising its institutional responsibilities. This core issue that teachers and others act "in the place of parents" is litigated in courts of law all the time. There seems to be a current movement away from stringent interpretations of this concept, but even if parents do win a legal battle on the basis of *in loco parentis*, such a victory is little consolation when their child is left forever affected by poor choices.

With so much at stake it is terribly important for parents to understand that their responsibility does not stop at the classroom door or at the wave good-bye as a neighbor drives off with their child to soccer practice. Why would parents be so casual about such things? There are probably a number of reasons, but I'd like to offer at least one for you to consider.

We live in an age of experts. Doctors specialize and subspecialize. We routinely consult sources of expertise for anything from dieting to marriage enhancement to cancer to stamp collecting to fundraising. In a culture that bows low to the expert, we have become accustomed to surrendering our minds and our rights in the presence of someone who occupies any position of supposed expertise. Teachers have gone to college, after all, so they must know what they are doing. Our son's music teacher played professionally for twenty years. I would not dream of telling him how to conduct a music lesson. I was never much of a soccer player and only slightly better at baseball. I guess my child's Little League coach knows what he is doing. After all, I heard he played in the Chicago Cubs farm system for a couple of years. And on it goes.

We quietly surrender our right to discern, our choice to risk conflict, and our ultimate responsibility before God every time we thoughtlessly turn our child over to the supervision of another. "But wait," you may be thinking. "Who can ever know for sure? How can I possibly shield my child from every possible bump and bruise? I'm not so sure that's a great idea anyway. Besides, I'd spend my whole life doing background checks and stalking music teachers to see what their private lives are like." Those are legitimate concerns. Let me see if I can address them as we close out chapter 1.

In reality, temperaments and parenting philosophies vary considerably among the most well-intentioned of parents. Therefore, my plea is not for parents to endorse a fail-safe formula for deciding whether we should hand our child over to another individual. My plea is more basic than that; it is for parents to recognize and then act upon their God-given responsibility to do their homework and to apply their own operative criteria for the benefit of their children.

What kind of homework do we have? Obviously I cannot anticipate every situation, but let me offer a few thoughts for your consideration. Communication is crucial. Talk with your child's music or dance teacher. Listen to your child carefully. Sit in on lessons regularly. Are you hearing reluctance or sadness about the lessons? My own musically gifted daughter cycled through a number of violin teachers during her teenage years. Most were good teachers in every sense of the word, but not all were appropriate for my daughter's temperament.

Spend the morning at your child's school. Watch how the teacher interacts with other children whose parents are not there to influence the situation. What is the general feel of the classroom? Talk to other parents of children in the class. Get to know your child's teacher.

When using a new babysitter, get references. Consider having the babysitter come to your home and spend the afternoon or evening with your children while you're present. Listen and observe the interaction.

Watch Little League practice. Watch in ways that allow your presence to be noted. Watch in more subtle ways. Linger after your child runs over to join his peers. Arrive early and quietly observe.

Talk to your child about his or her experience. What may seem harmless and benign to your eye may be getting processed quite differently by your child. You are in a position to know your child better than anyone, so keep your antennae up continuously.

Become an advocate on behalf of your children.

When you are truly engaged in your children's lives, you will have countless opportunities to help your child develop in crucial ways. When your boy strikes out at a critical point in the baseball game, this is a precious opportunity for you to emerge with a word of encouragement and wisdom. It will be your opportunity to put the situation in its proper perspective, and you can do it as no one else can. When your girl falters at the piano recital, this is your opportunity to support and shape and encourage in ways that only you can. And there may be times when you must rescue your child from an unhealthy situation.

In all cases, whatever is required by a particular circumstance, be there for your child! In other words, be engaged in the process. Get involved. Be informed. Know your child. Listen. Tune in. Pay attention. Act when necessary. God expects nothing less from us, having entrusted us with the precious and sacred gift of children. While we may share our children with various caregivers, we do not raise our children through committee rule. When it comes to your children, who is in charge here? By God's sovereign grace, you are.

Whatever you decide to do about your child's education, someone will disagree with your decision. It takes strength to stand firm. As you wrestle with the responsibilities associated with making this decision, I hope you will also draw strength from knowing that God not only expects you to act on his behalf for your child, he also stands ready to comfort, guide, and bless your efforts. With that in mind, let us now begin to explore the choices before us. We'll begin with public schools.

Why the Fuss?

I love school! I really do. I entered public school in 1950 and with the exception of two years in the 1980s I have been in the classroom ever since, either as a student or as a teacher. I taught fourth grade and sixth grade in public schools in Virginia for nearly ten years. A part of me still gets a sense of heightened anticipation every September as the weather begins to change; school has a rhythm that has gotten into my blood. Around September you can find school supplies in virtually every store. School buses begin to roll again. Marching bands begin rehearsing. Kids get new lunchboxes and wonder about new teachers. As the year unfolds students take tests, write papers, and make new friends. Teachers instruct, encourage, and periodically give out report cards. It is a rhythm marked by holidays, deadlines for work, successes, failures, and renewed efforts.

Although I did some of my graduate work at a Christian school, I am essentially a product of the public school system. My two daughters are products of the public school system too. I am fond of my experience with public schools, and while I have some negative things to say about them, I do so with sadness, not with malice.

I think it's important to note that public schools have been the target of criticism for at least fifty years. In 1955 Rudolph Flesch wrote his classic work, *Why Johnny Can't Read*, decrying the alleged failure of our public schools to teach America's children to read.[1] Over a quarter century later, Flesch wrote *Why Johnny Still Can't Read: A New Look at the Scandal of Our Schools*.[2]

In the late 1950s, the launching of the Russian satellite, Sputnik, sent Americans into a feverish examination of how America's schools had failed the country. And the concern was not only academic. I recall real incidents of violence in the schools I attended—students fighting in the halls and knocking teachers to the floor. The American school experience has always been a mixture of the national honor society, school newspaper projects, graffiti, glee club, pep rallies, bullies, crude sexual jokes, fundraisers, homecoming games, recess, and all the rest.

I was covering some of this material in a seminary course when one of my students spoke up in class. "I appreciate all the material you've been having us read. I've certainly learned a lot, and my eyes are open as never before. But I have my son in a public school first-grade classroom, and suddenly I feel as though I have the very breath of Satan on my neck for doing such a dastardly deed." I appreciated his comment. As far as he could tell, his son was doing just fine, and there did not seem to be any visible cause for concern.

In my efforts to sensitize my students to these issues, my voice had probably become too shrill. When this happens, I run the risk of losing people because I seem unrealistic in my analysis and out of control in my rhetoric. Eventually I will tell you that I believe the best choice for your child may be the public school. But I would not want you to make that choice without an informed understanding of what such a decision really means. So then, promising to keep my voice below the shrill level, let me share some sobering concerns I have about the public schools.

In the 1984–85 school year, which was my last year of public school teaching, I had a group of sixth graders. By then I was a seasoned veteran in the classroom and was not shocked by much. As I suggested earlier, problems in schools are not new. I resurfaced in the public school setting about six years later as a doctoral student supervising student teachers in Florida's public schools. I visited and supervised students in several counties and in a variety of socioeconomic settings. It didn't take me long to realize that things had deteriorated in the few intervening years.

I will never forget the day I sat in the back of a kindergarten class in one of the nicest suburban schools you could hope to send your child to and watched as a seemingly sweet little girl quietly but boldly raised her middle finger in an obscene gesture to a classmate across the room. "I don't think we're in Kansas anymore, Toto," I thought to myself. This was not a unique or isolated instance of aberrant behavior. In school after school after school, and at the elementary level no less, I was exposed to dismaying evidence of a malaise so pervasive and so complex that it was hard not to despair for our country.

I am not talking only about the world of inner-city schools. Many schools with major problems have modern facilities with libraries that boast freshly carpeted, sunken reading pits; classrooms in the round; reasonable student-teacher ratios; and computer labs that would impress the most technically savvy among us. It would feel almost blasphemous to say anything critical about these schools while you were in them because of how physically appealing they are. Yet, in spite of all the things money can buy, such schools are often riddled with problems that should be of deep concern to us as we try to decide what to do about the education and well-being of our children.

Is the name Michael Carneal familiar to you? At age fourteen, young Michael lived in a small town of twenty-seven thousand, where he played in his school band and was a B student. His father was a church deacon and a lawyer, and his older sister was valedictorian. Michael had never been in trouble and showed no evidence of distress. People still wonder what made this young resident of Paducah, Kentucky, carry a gun to school and kill three classmates back in 1997.[3]

In 1998 fifteen-year-old Kip Kinkel of Springfield, Oregon, first killed his parents and then went to school where he injured twenty-five students, two fatally.[4] The same year eleven-year-old Andrew Golden and his 13-year-old friend, Mitchell Johnson, residents of Jonesboro, Arkansas, went on a rampage at their school, killing five.[5] In April of 1998 fourteen-year-old Andrew Wurst allegedly killed a teacher at a school dance in Edinboro, Pennsylvania.[6] In May of 1998 Jacob Davis allegedly killed a classmate in the town of Fayetteville, Tennessee.[7] On April 20, 1999, Columbine High School was indelibly stamped on the consciousness of America when two students killed thirteen before taking their own lives.[8] Just over a year after the Columbine High School shooting, a thirteen-year-old boy in Florida brought a gun to school and killed a teacher in front of six other students.[9] I could mention more school shootings, but these are enough to make my point.

We are all shocked when we see a television news story about some child carrying a gun to school and opening fire on teachers and classmates. We are dumbfounded by these events, particularly as they seem to occur in places other than the inner city. It is not uncommon for these young killers to be small-town children from reasonably stable homes.

As unsettling and tragic as these events may be, we are tempted to think of them as isolated cases. After all, one or two incidents a year for an entire country is a minuscule percentage of the countless millions of children who go to school every day without incident. Are we unfairly citing a handful of the most extreme cases and making an unwarranted generalization about all schools? Is this what my seminary student was getting at? Let's look a little closer to see if we can answer this fair and important question.

In 1994, data compiled by the U.S. Department of Education showed that nearly one in four eighth-graders were involved in serious student fights.[10] Approximately one in five teachers were verbally abused, while 12 percent of teachers feared for their safety. A 1995 report from the National Center for Education Statistics indicated that one in four teachers in America rated physical conflicts among students as being serious or moderately serious problems in their schools.[11] These teachers are not reporting general misbehavior or bad attitudes or poor work habits. They are reporting physical conflicts.

Phi Delta Kappan, a highly respected professional journal of education, reported that an estimate of three million assorted crimes occur each year in the eighty-five thousand public schools in America.[12] This represents about 11 percent of all crime committed in the country. In the 1998 Phi Delta Kappa/Gallup Poll of the public's attitude toward public schools, parents were asked to indicate what they believed to be the biggest problem facing local schools.[13] Parents cited fighting and violence as the number one problem, with the lack of discipline and control not far behind. When asked if they feared for their child's physical safety while at school, over one-third of parents said yes.

Again, let me remind you that this is not an issue for those unfortunate enough to live in the inner city. A National School Board Association survey of seven hundred school districts nationwide reported that nearly 70 percent of rural (yes, rural) districts reported student assaults and fights as the most frequent type of violence.[14] Lyndon Furst, in the *Education Law Reporter*, stated, "The incidence of violent assault seems to occur at all strata of society and in all types of communities."[15]

It is tempting to list a continuous stream of alarming statistics about violence in our schools, but I think this is probably old news. The real danger, I believe, is to think that this is happening in the next school district or in the next county. If you have a child in a public school, you may not be hearing anything about these problems. You do not see much in the local papers and you see little evidence of a problem on your local news programs. Furthermore, your own child does not come home with stories about fights or other forms of violence.

Parents have a curious tendency to see problems as being "out there" somewhere, in the next district or the next county or the next state. We express a general concern, but we want to believe that our own child's school is an exception. This is born out by the results of the Phi Delta Kappa/Gallup Poll mentioned earlier.[16] When parents were asked to grade the nation's schools, only 16 percent gave a grade of A or B. When those same parents were asked to evaluate the school their child attended, 52 percent assigned a grade of A or B.

The everyday events of your child's school may not make the ten o'clock news, but that doesn't mean violence or serious disruption is not a problem in your area.

In your own school experience, do you recall a student fight making the local news? Of course not. If someone died or a lawsuit emerged, then the fight would become more newsworthy, but otherwise the media is not likely to report it.

This brings up a significant point about the severity of inappropriate school behavior. Misbehavior can range from the relatively benign spitball to a flagrant physical attack, which leaves a wide range of harmful behavior between the extremes. Are we concerned only with the life-or-death levels of misbehavior and violence? Can we all feel better because nobody has ever been stabbed or pushed down a flight of stairs at our children's schools?

Realistically, the average child in America's public schools will be exposed to a wide range of inappropriate behavior, even if the child is not directly involved. In the same study cited earlier, the National Center for Education Statistics reported over 70 percent of sixth through twelfth graders had personal knowledge of bullying, physical attack, or robbery at their schools.[17]

What effect does witnessing violence have on youth? The American Psychological Association Commission on Violence and Youth stated that "even youth who are not direct victims of violence may be victimized by the chronic presence of violence in their communities."[18] Without trying to measure or analyze the impact this kind of exposure has on our children's values and emotional well-being, we can safely agree to the obvious impact on learning. Albert Shanker, former president of the American Federation of Teachers, rightly observes, "You can deliver a terrific curriculum, but if youngsters are throwing things, cursing and yelling and punching each other, the curriculum doesn't mean a thing in that classroom."[19]

Earlier I asked if you can recall from your own experience a school fight ever making the evening news. I assumed your answer was no. I also want to ask whether you recall going home and telling your parents about a school fight. With some exceptions of course, I suspect few acts of violence get reported at home.

Most students don't think it's necessary to report misbehavior to Mom and Dad. It becomes such a part of school culture that expecting children to inform their parents would be like asking fish to become aware of the water in which they live. You ask your dear one, "How was your day?" and the answer is likely to be "Okay" or "Fine." You can probe and prod, which I strongly encourage, but you still may not get a realistic picture of your child's school-day experience. For example, a survey on sexual harassment reported that of students who had been sexually harassed by a teacher or other school personnel, 61 percent did not tell their parents.[20] If the source of harassment was a fellow student, 83 percent of the time the victim did not tell a parent. When students did tell someone, they were much more likely to tell a friend.

I'm afraid there is more. Having brought up this matter of sexual harassment, let's pause for a moment and look at that issue. I promise not to linger too long here, but this is a matter of real importance. To follow are a few quick snapshots to give you a feel for the scope of the problem:

- Between 1985 and 1990 there were 145 teachers in California who lost their licenses to teach because of sexual misconduct with students.[21]
- The youngest child to file and win a sexual harassment case was a girl named Cheltzie in 1992. She was six years old.[22]

- Research suggests that neither race, ethnicity, parents' education, nor academic standing are associated with the likelihood of being sexually harassed.[23]
- This is not only a female issue. Approximately 60 percent of high school boys receive unwanted sexual attention.[24] For example, during the 1993–94 school year in Connecticut, 57 percent of male students reported that they had been the targets of unwelcome sexual conduct since they started high school.[25]
- From a much-discussed *Seventeen* magazine survey, we read that in a group of nine to twelve-year-olds, 77 percent reported they had been touched, pinched, or grabbed in a sexual manner. Twenty percent said they had been "pressured to do something sexual." Thirty-nine percent reported some form of sexual harassment directed at them daily, with an additional 29 percent reporting an average occurrence of one episode per week.[26]
- More teachers in America lose their licenses to teach for sexually abusing children than for any other reason.[27] A four-year study involving 225 cases of students being sexually abused by teachers or professional staff revealed more incidents at the elementary school level than the high school level.[28]

Just as in the case of school violence, headline-grabbing incidents of sexual misconduct tend to be the most offensive and most dramatic occurrences. Unfortunately, a wide range of sexual misconduct takes place in our schools that never makes the news but should be just as much a cause for concern and parental vigilance.

Consider this partial definition of sexual harassment offered by Irwin Hyman, professor of school psychology at Temple University. He says it includes "leering, pinching, grabbing, suggestive verbal comments, pressure for sexual activity, spreading sexual rumors, making sexual or sexist jokes, pulling at another student's clothing, cornering or brushing up against a student in a sexual way."[29] This is the stuff of daily school life, and as reported in one of the snapshots earlier, it does not seem to matter whether you are educated, live in a nice neighborhood, and have a bright achieving child.

Because this less dramatic sort of behavior is such a familiar part of the school experience, you're not likely to hear about it from your child. Even if your son or daughter is fortunate enough to escape being a direct target of these disturbing behaviors, it will be all around them in one form or another. A child who swims in this soup every day accepts the status quo. The impact on values, attitudes, and emotional well-being is incalculable.

I've given a brief summary of the problems of sex and violence in our schools. I won't go into the same detail about the problem of alcohol and drug consumption, but in one survey 70 percent of public school students and 52 percent of private school students, ages twelve to nineteen, reported that drugs were available at their schools.[30]

Overwhelming as these statistics are, somehow we have to take a deep breath and make eye contact with the reality of this problem. I do not know where you live, but it does not seem to matter when it comes to the concerns being discussed. I can say with confidence that these issues, in their many forms, have taken up residence in your neighborhood and will find expression in your schools.

We need to understand that a relationship exists between school culture and culture at large. In your local community, people are waking up each morning, in houses and apartments up and down every street. They will each follow their morning routine, and from many of these homes children will emerge and head off to a school building. The building is just so much brick, wood, plumbing, and the rest. But as teachers and students and custodians and secretaries and principals and counselors arrive, it becomes school. School is not an autonomous institution that is somehow separate from the people who make up the institution. To the extent that school culture consists of violence, sexual misconduct, drugs, and all the rest, we should see it as a reflection of the culture outside of the school building.

Every individual school represents a collection of diverse people attempting to function in a community. The educational effort would be challenging enough if all the players shared the same outlook on life, had the same background and experiences, the same value system, the same gracious acceptance of others, or if no one ever had a headache or needed sleep or was ever distracted by life's many problems. Of course, things aren't this simple, so life at school is even more challenging.

Another point to consider is that each school conducts business amid certain realities such as building space, class size, and the administrative policies typically found in a school context. The net result is sometimes less than ideal. Let me explain what I mean in the next chapter.

So Much Time,
So Little Learning!

Aaaaarrggghhh! That is the sound you are likely to hear from me on Tuesdays, Thursdays, and Saturdays. For the first time in my life I have joined an exercise health club. I am learning all sorts of things about exercise, physical fitness, and even a bit about pain.

I am also learning some unexpected things about what it means to be a part of a fitness club. For example, I have learned what kind of clothing is "cool" and what is marginally acceptable. I have learned how much eye contact with other exercisers is appropriate, when it is alright to speak to them, and the fine art of looking into mirrored walls without appearing to look. I am learning how to wait for someone to finish on a piece of equipment. This is a delicate art consisting of appropriate distance, a stance that does not directly face the other person, and a courteous moment of eye contact, the duration of which has to be felt rather than explained.

These and a host of other bits of exercise club protocol are part of what I am learning in order to get back into good physical condition. In fact, you could say that there is a self-contained cultural ethos at the health club that is built around norms, values, and expectations. It is an adventure, because virtually none of these behavioral norms are listed as rules on the wall, and the employees do not feel it is necessary to explain them. Schools are like that. Let me explain what I mean, and in the process I'll tell you why this is so important to understand.

Among teachers, conventional wisdom is that posted, written rules should be kept to a minimum. There is no way to anticipate every situation that may occur during a typical school day, along with the possible exceptions, so it makes sense to keep written lists to a minimum. Consider the example of something simple, like the classroom protocol for sharpening a pencil. If the teacher is giving instructions or illustrating something at the chalkboard, this is probably not an acceptable time for students to get out of their seats and create the noise that is a part of sharpening pencils. When the class is involved in completing a written assignment, some teachers may or may not permit students to sharpen their pencils. Other teachers may set limits of two students at a time at the pencil sharpener. Some require that students raise their hands to get permission, while others allow certain liberties under certain circumstances. Others may hope to avoid the whole issue by requiring students to have multiple pencils at their desks, and they are allowed to sharpen pencils only at the beginning of the day. Even with established norms that govern the pencil-sharpening protocol of a given classroom, there are always exceptions that may occur depending on the mood of the teacher, the perceived trustworthiness of a given student, and how intrusive the sound of the sharpener will be at a given moment. It is impossible to write a rule for every possible pencil-sharpening scenario, and this is but one small segment of a typical school day. The situation becomes even more complex when you consider how many relatively insignificant actions are governed by a similar unwritten code of conduct.

Students learn what is necessary to negotiate a trip to the restroom. There are protocols for asking the teacher a question or soliciting help from a classmate. Students learn where the acceptable noise-level thresholds are, and how those levels vary depending on the time of day, mood of the teacher, nature of the activity, the weather outside, number of students in the room at the time, and numerous other mediating conditions. As you can see, the public school classroom is a complex, interactive, ever-changing, organic culture.

This is never so apparent as when students have a substitute teacher. You remember how it was. The poor substitute did not know any of the unwritten rules. She did not count the lunch money on time. She let the boys go first. She had students pass their homework forward, instead of having the helper-of-the-day collect it. She got angry because three of the girls did not ask permission to go to a listening center in the room (as they always did when the regular teacher was there). Ten minutes did not go by before the well-meaning substitute teacher would violate an unwritten expectation.

An important question to ask is, Why are these protocols necessary? I would argue they are necessary because any time you put twenty to thirty children in a room, you create an environment in which education is impossible without them. Even with firmly established protocols, is the public school classroom the best environment for education?

Let's imagine a fourth-grade classroom in which the teacher has just instructed her class to put away their science books and get out their math books. This simple activity can chew up amazing amounts of time. Why? Ralph, Melinda, and Kurt didn't hear their teacher tell them to make the switch, so they are already lagging behind. Prompt students will wait for those three. The clock ticks while everyone waits for these three. Veronica pulled her math notebook out from under her desk, causing all the other books and papers to spill onto the floor. This caused a certain amount of laughter among those around her, which in turn has caused others to stop their activity to see what the fuss is about.

The clock ticks as at least ten students have paused to ask what is so funny. We all wait for Veronica to express her dismay and pick everything up and put it away. The teacher and the class wait. Jeremy can't find his math notebook at all and suspects that Brandon has once again pulled his trick of swiping a book from Jeremy's desk to place into someone else's desk. What a laugh that is. Jeremy always loses it when this happens! Everyone is invited to double-check their desks for an extra math notebook. Tick-tock. Eventually everyone has their math notebooks and that little task is accomplished.

Time elapsed? Three minutes? Seven minutes? Nine minutes? It will vary depending on type and number of distractions, mood and experience of the teacher, and any number of other factors. Remember that there are five or six subjects in a day, and you begin to understand how much time is wasted. Nevertheless, if it were only a matter of a few minutes between subjects, we probably would be tempted to shrug our shoulders and figure that this is a small price to pay to educate so many children in one room. But the story continues.

The teacher is finally ready to begin the thirty-five-to-forty-minute math lesson, having lost approximately five minutes to get the students ready to begin. Into the lesson at last, the teacher pauses as the announcement for the school's fundraising candy sales is made over the public address system. As the announcement fades, a conversational buzz results as several students feel compelled to tell their friends how many candy bars their moms sold at work.

During this interruption the teacher notices Sylvia has a pained look on her face. A brief conversation reveals Sylvia does not feel well, so the teacher invites her to put her head down on her desk to see if she can shake it off. Approximately ten minutes back into the lesson, Ralph drops his book onto the floor. Laughter. Tick. Interruption for note-passing incident. Tock. Student photo day. Broken pencil. What page are we on? Tick. Sylvia just got sick on the floor. Get rid of that gum, Leslie. Tock. Commotion in the hall. Vickie, would you mind shutting the door? Tick tock.

Every interruption chews up time, and the class waits. Because this is a group enterprise, the class either moves or waits together. Diligent students stop, and wait. Is that your son or daughter sitting in the third seat, row two, waiting? Bright students wait, lose interest, lose focus, and get pulled into the distraction of the moment. One can only speculate about the cumulative effect this has on the motivation and interest of students.

I'm not exaggerating. Ten years in the classroom taught me there is no end to distractions and interruptions. While there are the occasional discipline problems that may bring instruction to a halt, I am intentionally not talking about those kinds of time-consuming activities. The large majority of the interruptions are benign in the sense that there is no deliberate intent on the part of students or school officials to undermine the educational effort. These time eaters are simply an inescapable reality of mass education.

I have come to believe that one measure of a good teacher is his or her ability to reduce wasted time to a minimum, but I also know, as every veteran teacher does, that doing so is comparable to warfare. Because the teacher and students must operate in the context of a group (or parts of groups), everything takes longer. Getting thirty students to line up for lunch or music or art or buses or anything else takes much longer than getting four or five students to do the same. This is true even if there is no misbehavior involved.

Our country's commitment to educate every single child in the U.S. is a great testament to the American spirit, but doing so involves inescapable logistical problems. Much time is simply lost in the effort, and this time must ultimately be taken from the only source available, which is time that would have been given to instruction. This brings me to another concern.

Interruptions and logistical issues can reduce real instruction significantly. A thirty-five-minute lesson may only amount to half that time of actual teaching. Although I suspect many parents would be shocked to learn how little instruction takes place during a typical school day, teachers have understood this frustrating reality for some time. Researchers have observed and recorded the way time is spent in the typical classroom, and the results are sobering.

In a review of research on what makes teachers and schools effective, James Bauman emphasizes how important it is for students to spend "time on task."[1] In other words, students need to stay focused on the task at hand, without the many distractions already described. The enemies of time on task are "transition times, talking, disciplining, and the like." Researcher Robert Gaskins offers this observation:

> In many of the classrooms, caring and conscientious teachers tended to allow poor readers to spend an alarming amount of time in unproductive ways. For example,

it was not uncommon for a teacher to call a reading group to the reading table and allow 5 to 10 minutes to elapse before the lesson began. This time lapse often resulted from students' slow, conversation-ridden journeys to the reading table, as well as lack of readiness on the part of the teacher to begin the reading lesson.[2]

In another study, researchers examined the use of time for 132 elementary school teachers in six different schools.[3] The conclusions were quite similar. Of the six hours spent at school, teachers and students spent only a third of the day on instructional tasks. The researchers noted, "Transitions, that is, moving from one activity to another, were the single most frequent cause for reducing allocated academic time while in the classroom." There were, however, many more activities that impeded instruction. The list of interruptions included fire drills, counselor sessions, errands, trips to the school office, late buses, worksheet distribution, collecting homework, roll call, collecting money, student confusion, unavailability of materials, announcements, clarification of classroom rules, going to lunch, going to the restroom, and waiting.

This is just a sampling of the observations that educational researchers have made about life in the classroom. We are not talking about bomb scares or fist fights in the back of the room. This is business-as-usual stuff, everyday life for our public school students.

Making the classroom a more "Christian" environment isn't going to help these problems. You could institute prayer in schools, post the Ten Commandments on the walls, and place a born-again Christian teacher in every classroom, and nothing of substance would change regarding the problems I have described. Christian or not, virtually all of us are the products of years of this kind of experience. Many of us have become numb to the inescapable waste of time and weak instruction that occurs in our efforts to mass-educate America's enormous population of school-age children.

How bad is America's education? We've all heard reports about how poorly American test scores fare when compared to those of other countries. You probably have heard about teachers who are unable to pass the most basic tests of knowledge or competency. I won't go into detail about these issues, but I do want to cover the events of April 26, 1983.

In 1981 the United States Secretary of Education, Terrel H. Bell, established a commission of approximately eighteen educators to study the condition of education in America.[4] The commission, according to Bell, was "selected to be broadly representative of American education and of the geographic, racial, and ethnic diversity of the country." The commission consisted of a Nobel Prize winner, several university presidents, a corporate executive, local school board presidents, and a host of other noteworthy educators. On April 26, two years later, this commission tendered their report to Congress.

To this day educators continue to talk about, critique, and adjust policy as a result of this report, which was ominously titled, "A Nation at Risk: The Imperative for Educational Reform." Only thirty-six pages long, its conclusions and language were explosive. Space does not permit a full exposition of this report, but consider these brief excerpts:

> Our nation is at risk. Our once unchallenged preeminence in commerce, industry, science, and technological innovation is being overtaken by competitors throughout the world.

The educational foundations of our society are presently being eroded by a rising tide of mediocrity that threatens our very future as a nation and a people.

If an unfriendly foreign power had attempted to impose on America the mediocre educational performance that exists today, we might well have viewed it as an act of war.

These are strong words! Please note these are not the observations of a group of militant dogmatists with an ax to grind. Nor do they come from someone outside of the system lobbing flamboyant missiles to gain fifteen minutes of fame. These are the words of in-house, eminent educators, genuinely concerned about our children. Much has transpired since the original report was issued, including several legislative/financial initiatives designed to correct perceived deficiencies. However, because many of the problems are simply a function of the way America does school, the concerns are as real today as they were when the report was submitted in 1983.

Ten years after the report was issued, Emeral A. Crosby, one of the original report's commissioners, observed that "we still lack the will and the commitment to reduce the risks that imperil our children."[5] I would argue that nothing of substance has changed since the report was submitted to Congress. How weak is the instruction at your local school? Weak enough that you should be truly concerned.

The causes of our public school malaise are many, and they are often complex. I have mentioned serious issues such as sexual abuse and violence in our schools, which undoubtedly impact the quality of instruction in our schools. But the story of our public school system is about more than incompetence or abuse. Less shocking, but conditions inherent in the educational system should concern us as well.

The logistics of trying to manage a classroom of twenty-five to thirty-five children make quality instruction a major challenge for every hard-working teacher. Even if your child is heading off each morning to a nice suburban school with the smell of new carpet still noticeable, a sunken reading pit, computers in every classroom, diligent teachers, a strong PTA, teacher's aides in every room, everyone feeling well and having no personal problems, and anything else you want to add, instructional obstacles are still a reality of mass education. They are inescapably a part of the way the State attempts to educate our children.

Beyond the Three R's

What You Really Learn in School

If you were to walk into a school classroom and ask a teacher to describe her curriculum to you, the teacher is likely to produce the textbooks used in class and leaf through the pages pointing out the various topics covered. Referring to her lesson-plan book, she might talk about the current unit being covered and how it fits with the rest the curriculum. Once she covers the specifics of her classroom material, she might talk about extracurricular activities—chess club, debate team, yearbook staff, chorus—that are available to students. However, a large segment of the curriculum is not likely to get mentioned.

Whereas textbooks, worksheets, microscopes and other hardware, and lesson plans are the tangible evidence of the official curriculum, another curriculum is hidden from view. This hidden curriculum is arguably more important and farther reaching than the official curriculum and has caught the attention of a number of researchers and educators in recent years. In the last chapter I made the point that a good deal of time is wasted during the school day. It is perhaps a bit misleading to refer to that as noninstructional time, because lessons are being learned in the midst of disruption and waiting. This is the stuff of the hidden curriculum. Let me explain.

Imagine young Briana sitting in her classroom working on a worksheet when her only pencil breaks. Aware that she is expected to have extra pencils sharpened in her desk, she must now attempt to negotiate the pencil-sharpening protocol set by Mrs. Hammond, the teacher. Sizing up her teacher's apparent mood as she grades papers at her desk, Briana decides on a course of action. Sliding quietly from her desk, she softly approaches Mrs. Hammond's desk with her broken pencil.

Stopping several feet from her teacher she tentatively holds her pencil forth and whispers, "I'm sorry, Mrs. Hammond." There is a moment of hesitation and then the wordless nod of the head lets Briana know that her violation of the standard rule is acceptable, and she is soon back to work. It was a simple exchange, yet Briana has learned far more than meets the eye. What has Briana learned from this piece of the hidden curriculum?

There are rules, and Briana has been learning that rules seem to govern much of life. She also has learned that there are consequences for breaking rules, although it gets a little vague at this point. Apparently rules can be broken if you play your cards right. Of course it is important to read the teacher's mood correctly and to pick the right tone of voice and body language when approaching her. Along the way Briana has observed that her classmate, Paul, seems to incur Mrs. Hammond's wrath for breaking the same rule, no matter how he tries to deal with the situation. Sometimes Briana can tell what Paul is doing wrong when he approaches Mrs. Hammond, but other times it is not discernible.

She is beginning to think her teacher does not like Paul very much.

This makes Briana sad because she likes her teacher, but she likes Paul too. She is learning lessons about life and people, about inequity and fairness, and about how to make situations work to your advantage. Multiply this scenario by countless dozens of seemingly small transactions throughout a school day, and you have the content of the hidden curriculum. Incidentally, the lessons have not been lost on Paul either.

Could it be that Mrs. Hammond really does not like Paul? If you really knew Mrs. Hammond, you would find that hard to believe. A mother herself, one of her own children attends this same school. A professional through and through with fourteen years of teaching under her belt, Mrs. Hammond just this past spring finished the last course for her master's degree at the local university. She is a faithful Sunday school teacher at her church, and growing out of her religious convictions is a conscious determination to treat every child fairly and with dignity. Is Briana's perception that Mrs. Hammond treats Paul differently correct? As painful or unnerving as it may be, the answer is likely to be yes.

As we unpack the depth of the hidden curriculum, let's consider the dramatic events that took place many years ago at Oak School in California. As the 1964–65 school year began at Oak School, teachers were given a list of their students for the year. Sprinkled throughout the lists of names were special designations identifying certain students as academically gifted. This label was assigned to children who scored in the top 20 percent on a Harvard test intended to measure academic ability. These students were scattered throughout the school; some teachers had only one of these promising students, while other teachers had as many as nine.

Using a series of tests throughout the year, administrators evaluated the academic progress of these special students. As you might expect, they did indeed show academic progress and advancement that exceeded that of classmates who were not identified as academically gifted. IQ and reading scores, for example, were noticeably higher for these special students. Seems reasonable, doesn't it? Why have these results given birth to decades of debate and research that continue to this day?

I have left out a few key pieces of information. You see, this was actually a grand experiment in which the alleged gifted students were in fact randomly selected and actually no more capable than any of their classmates.[1] The teachers were led to believe, through the original class roll, that certain students were more capable than others. As the researchers wrote, "The difference between the special children and the ordinary children, then, was only in the mind of the teacher." It is worth noting, in light of the results, that the so-called special children were scattered throughout the entire school, from grades one through six. How do we begin to explain such a startling phenomenon?

Apparently, what teachers think about students, even at the most subtle levels, somehow gets communicated to the students in a way that is powerful enough to impact their success or failure in school and, by extension, in life! It seems attitudes and expectations from the teacher leak to students, and students pick up on these signals in a way that makes them work harder or not as hard. The implications are far reaching and have captured the imagination of researchers for decades. For example, twenty-five years later researchers examined the student performance of 1,731 sixth-grade students in light of their teachers' expectations. It was found that "the more favorably teachers viewed students in October, the more those students increased their grades and standardized test scores above the levels predicted by prior performance and motivation."[2]

What is unsettling about all of this is not the idea that teachers can inspire good work in their students. Rather, it is the fact that teachers apparently do this in ways that are neither conscious nor deliberate. You can be sure that teachers in the Oak School study and in many other studies since have been as surprised by the results as you and I. Unaware of their subtle behaviors, they have nevertheless communicated powerful messages of expectation to their students.

Perhaps even more disturbing is the evidence that teachers do this unevenly. Not all students receive the same positive, high-expectation messages that would lead them to do their best work. As researchers tried to discover how teachers communicate these attitudes toward their students, a fascinating, if not disturbing, portrait of life in our schools emerged.

Did you ever get teased at school? Perhaps you were a bit chubby, had freckles, wore glasses, had braces on your teeth, were tall or short for your age, or any number of other possible reasons children tease each other. Hopefully this does not bring up painful memories, but my point is that we're all aware that teasing is a part of life in school. We may be inclined to think it's harmless and even a part of learning to get on in life. And we may be right, unless in fact this teasing leads to being treated in more or less preferential ways, which in turn leads to success or failure in school.

It is no secret that our culture places a premium on attractive people, whether the context is Hollywood, the business world, advertising, or the street. Extensive research in many fields has shown that we are all inclined to attribute certain positive characteristics to physically attractive people, even when we know nothing about a person. If a false test score can influence teachers' expectations of their students' academic ability, could nonacademic factors like physical appearance do the same?

The answer appears to be yes. In one study over four hundred elementary school teachers were given cumulative folders for all their students.[3] Each folder contained a photograph of an attractive or unattractive child and a report of academic ability. Each student was presented as a B student, so the only variation in any of the folders was the attached photograph. Based on nothing more than a photograph, teachers rated the attractive children as (1) more intelligent, (2) having higher academic potential, and (3) having parents with a higher interest in education. It is worth pointing out that the responses were not of a general nature whereby teachers seemed to "like" attractive children a bit more than unattractive children. Teachers actually attributed academic qualities and family characteristics to these children on the sole basis of their physical appearance. In case we are feeling inclined to think too negatively toward teachers for this seemingly unprofessional behavior, it should be pointed out that this sort of phenomenon is found in all of us.

At East Carolina University, 144 undergraduates were asked to make similar observations of adult men and women from photographs.[4] They too found the more attractive people to be more likely to be more capable. In a completely different scenario, experimenters planted an apparently lost graduate school application in a public phone booth. Attached to the packet was a photograph of an attractive or unattractive applicant. Guess which packets got mailed most frequently. If you said those with photos of attractive applicants, you were right.

Photographs were also used to measure reaction to people wearing glasses. For example, one study revealed that faces with spectacles are perceived as less attractive, less friendly, more shy, and meaner.[5] Children are not immune to these subtle influences either. Using fourth grade boys and girls as judges, it was found that they rated those wearing glasses as less attractive, more likely to do poorly in school and to misbehave in the classroom.[6]

Even mothers are susceptible to the influence of physical appearance and the judgments they make about children. In one experiment, mothers rated larger boys as more competent than average or small boys.[7] They associated height with competence on tasks of logical ability among boys. In the same study, it was determined that mothers punished small girls less than tall girls. But it doesn't end here. Those things that might influence a teacher's attitude toward a child are not limited to physical appearance.

School teachers were given student essays and asked to assign a grade.[8] What they did not know was that the essays had been screened so that they were all judged to be of generally equal quality. However, one set of these essays consistently got better grades. How could this be, if the essays were already determined to be of equal quality? The answer was handwriting. The essays with poorer handwriting consistently received lower grades even though handwriting was not part of the official evaluation process.

In a separate experiment involving student essays, researchers wanted to see if teachers would grade student papers differently based on something even less related to academic ability.[9] In a manner similar to the handwriting study, experienced teachers were given short student essays already judged by others to be of comparable quality. All essays should have received the same grade, but again the grades were consistently lower for a certain portion of those evaluated. The difference this time? Name of child. For half the essays there was assigned a male or female name considered to be currently popular. For the other half of the essays, the name at the top of the page was considered to be a currently unpopular name, such as Bertha or Elmer. Guess which essays received the lower grades? And you thought Bertha and Elmer only suffered socially. Unless you've felt the burden of your own unusual name, you might be surprised at how important something like a first name can be.

Just as we tend to form impressions of people on the basis of their height or weight or various mannerisms, apparently we are significantly influenced by names. Even the use of a formal version of a name, such as Robert instead of Bob, can cause people to alter their judgments of others.[10] Robert is thought to be less extroverted, more conscientious, more emotionally stable, and more cultured than those using either Bob or Bobby. Unconventionally spelled versions of common names are viewed negatively.[11] Lynda is more likely to be associated with lower levels of success, morality, popularity, warmth, and cheerfulness than would be her friend Linda.

The popularity of elementary school children has been correlated with the popularity or unpopularity of their names.[12] In a fascinating study, 197 college students were asked to vote on a beauty queen from among six photographs, all judged to be equivalent in physical attractiveness, as determined by rankings of thirty-five students from a separate university.[13] They randomly assigned desirable and undesirable names to the photographs and then tallied the votes. Kathy, Jennifer, and Christine received 47, 52, and 59 votes respectively. Ethel, Harriet, and Gertrude received 11, 14, and 14 votes, even though all were considered to be equally attractive.

As unnerving as all of this is, it should not come as a complete shock to us. All of us learn to read the nuances of behavior and appearance in others. In many ways this is how we try to discern the trustworthiness of another person and whether or not we desire to have further contact with that person. In many cases our first impressions have a far-reaching impact. For example, rightly or wrongly, studies show potential employers often make their decision to hire or not to hire within the first four minutes of an interview.[14] This decision is based on a combination of factors ranging from dress to duration of eye contact to body tilt to voice inflection.

We have experts teaching us how to dress for success, so our physical appearance will maximize the positive impression we make. Salesmen learn how much eye contact to sustain, how to move closer to the client when asking for a favorable decision, and how hard it is to say no to a request when you are being touched by the requester. Waitresses learn how to increase their tips by the use of eye contact, nonintrusive touch, and the offering of their first names. Lawyers learn how to present their clients in the most favorable way. Jurors want to be able to see witnesses in person, to look into their eyes, and to watch the way they answer questions. What mother has not gotten down on eyeball level with her child to insist on the truth? Mothers practice intuitively what researchers have found scientifically: it is harder to lie when making eye contact.

All of these studies suggest human communication and the formation of impressions is a complex phenomenon. Teachers, being human, are just as vulnerable to being influenced by nonacademic factors as any other segment of our population. This truth was brought home to me in a very personal way several years ago

57

when I was teaching fourth grade at a public school in Virginia.

Darnell was a pain. While I do not believe I reacted to Darnell because of his size or handwriting or other possible influences mentioned in this chapter, I nevertheless formed some impressions of Darnell that eventually took over our relationship. I won't bore you with the details, but suffice it to say his obnoxious behavior pushed all the wrong buttons in me. For months he and I did the teacher-student dance of defiance and discipline. I remember moving him all over the room in an attempt to get him under control—beside my desk, in the back corner. I even tried putting his desk in the hall. Nothing worked.

Of course, the whole time I was conducting myself in the most exemplary manner, or so I wanted to believe. Surely my demeanor was consistent no matter whom I was dealing with. My voice and body language did not change whether I was making pleasant conversation with high-achiever Suzy or dealing with Darnell's disruptive behavior. It was, after all, important for the students to know that I cared for all of them equally. I really believed this, as I think most teachers do!

As the weeks turned into months, something was eating at me about this situation. The first flicker of insight came as I was taking attendance one morning. Checking the seating chart, I came to Darnell's desk and saw that he was absent. The private elation was undeniable. I knew that my whole day was going to be different because Darnell was gone. At the emotional level I wanted to celebrate. The conviction that followed was equally undeniable.

Within days I deliberately moved toward Darnell instead of away from him. One day we walked out to recess together, and instead of him running off to play, we wandered around the playground together, talking.

I asked about Darnell's brothers and sisters, and without prying I learned a good bit about the problems he was enduring at home. Within the space of an hour I gained tremendous insight into Darnell's behavior. I went to recess seeing Darnell as a problem to be solved. I returned seeing Darnell as a needy human being. Somehow that seemed to change everything. Even though we continued to struggle for the rest of the school year, it was clear that Darnell was picking up on my changed attitudes, and his behavior was much improved.

For the first time, I began to wonder about the veneer of professionalism I thought I was maintaining. If Darnell was picking up on my attitude toward him, what were the other students picking up? As it turns out, children read adults (including teachers) very perceptively. Consider the following.

Five groups of judges were selected, consisting of fourth-graders, seventh-graders, tenth-graders, teachers-in-training, and experienced teachers.[15] The judges were exposed to a video of a teacher talking to or about a student for whom the teacher had either high or low expectations. The viewer could not see the student in question or anything other than the speaker's head. The speaker did not explicitly state anything about his or her expectations for the student. Some of the judges saw the video and heard no sound. Others heard the sound and saw no video. A third group had the benefit of both sound and video.

In each case judges of all ages were able to determine the academic excellence of the student based on how the teacher spoke to or about the student. Also, judges were able to determine the extent to which the teacher was fond of the student. If we stopped there, the results would be dramatic enough. Even the group who could not hear the teacher and the group who could not see the teacher were able to determine biases.

This is not, however, the most unsettling dimension of the study. In each case the judges were exposed to the video for only ten seconds! These findings prompted the authors of this study to declare, "Very fine nuances in teacher behavior—many of which are nonverbal, uncontrollable, unconscious, and often undetected in natural observation—seem to have substantial, accumulating effects on students."

The reality is that teachers are not fooling anyone. The children know whom teachers consider to be an annoyance, and they pick up on the uneven treatment this produces. They know if there is a teacher's pet. They know whom the teacher believes are smart children, and they know where they fit in that hierarchy. As we have seen, this is not a matter of teachers having a harmless preference. As teacher opinion is translated into expectations, it impacts everything from self-esteem to academic achievement on the part of students. Even when academic quality is high, students can be graded lower for reasons that have more to do with teacher expectation than with actual student performance.

While teachers are often unaware of their biased expectations, students learn that this is a reality of life in the classroom. The lessons learned in school reach well beyond the formal, stated curriculum typically found in textbooks. In fact, the less direct lessons of the hidden curriculum may be more important than any math or reading or science lesson.

I have vivid memories of getting my fourth-graders to memorize their multiplication tables. There were no shortcuts, and I was acutely aware of the real disadvantage children would have if they did not master their multiplication tables at this point in their schooling. I set up an elaborate system of rewards for those who mastered this laborious exercise in rote memorization. What did my children learn as they wrestled with these multiplication facts? Sure, they learned that 7 times 8 is 56, but they learned a lot more than multiplication tables.

I like the observations of education philosopher William Kilpatrick who said, "Whether we like it or not, whether we know it or not, a child learning multiplication tables is also at the same time learning something about dawdling and not dawdling."[16] In one way or another, children are also learning whether or not they like arithmetic, how they feel about school in general, the teacher, peer pressure, their parents, and the virtue of hard work. A child in my class might wonder if all learning is something one has to be bribed to undertake.

Catherine Cornbleth raises another concern:

Many students . . . seem to be adept at "playing school," that is keeping up appearances and seeming to go along in order to gain advantage without internalizing the school's values or views of the world. Others may develop sophisticated forms of defiance, enabling them to avoid both subordination to school norms and getting into trouble with school authorities. They approach their school situation in ways not unlike the speeding motorist on the lookout for radar traps; instead of becoming more law abiding, they become more adept at law breaking.[17]

Is this the grand lesson of school? Are we teaching our children merely how to cope, how to navigate through the intricate world of the hidden curriculum without losing too much of their good sense or personal integrity? Some, like John Gatto, New York State Teacher of the Year in 1991, would put it even more strongly. Gatto says that "we need to realize that the school institution 'schools' very well, though it does not educate" and "schools teach exactly what they are intended to teach and they do it well: how to be a good Egyptian and remain in your place in the pyramid."[18] Twenty-six years of public school teaching in Manhattan led this articulate, award-winning teacher to conclude, "It is time that we squarely face the fact that institutional school teaching is destructive to children." He is not criticizing bad math lessons, a weak geography curriculum, or a reading program with an ineffective emphasis. What Gatto is talking about is the impact of all the lessons of the hidden curriculum.

Another award-winning teacher has made a similar, albeit more gently put, observation. Several years ago Minnesotan Guy Doud was selected to receive the National Teacher of the Year Award from among all the public school teachers in America. He stated that, "In school, the most profound lessons you learn are the lessons you learn about yourself."[19] He too recognized that school was much more than math and science lessons, learning state capitals, how to write a proper sentence, and all the rest of the formal, stated curriculum. These honored, devoted public school teachers have helped us all to see the scope and power of the hidden curriculum.

Studying the particulars of the hidden curriculum is a bit like peeling an onion. The hidden curriculum covers a wide range of matters from work ethic to interpersonal behavior to peer pressure to self perception to attitude toward authority to the appropriateness of humor to honesty to a sense of fair play, and a myriad of other lessons that we learn along the way toward becoming an adult.

I should point out that not everything learned from the hidden curriculum is negative. School is where many of us learned at least in part what it means to take your proper turn, to be punctual with assignments, or to help a struggling friend. However, in the same school where children may be learning positive lessons from the hidden curriculum, they also may be learning that cheating is one of the ways you survive, making fun of the chubby girl in class seems to raise your stock among certain popular peers, and misbehavior only has consequences if you are caught. The lessons of the hidden curriculum are often a mixture of positive and negative influences on your child's development.

Parents will never know or be able to control all the lessons of the hidden curriculum that take place during the course of a typical school day. This does not excuse them, however, from doing their very best to help children navigate through these difficult waters. Peter Hlebowitsh cautions teachers about the importance of the hidden curriculum when he says, "The fundamental point is that collateral learning will always be operating and that we educators ignore it at our peril."[20]

Perhaps this chapter has raised some concerns. If so, you probably have some questions. How is a parent to be responsible about these issues when the hidden curriculum is, well, hidden? Even if parents knew their children were learning lessons during simple procedures like lining up for lunch or from asking to go to the school clinic or from practical jokes, how could parents possibly control such lessons?

These are legitimate questions. And in view of earlier material concerning school violence, sexual harassment, amount of time wasted, and the effects of teacher expectations, it is clear any mother and father desiring the very best for their children need help. For this reason, our discussion now turns to ways parents can help their child not only survive but hopefully flourish in their educational setting.

The Parental Factor

As you might imagine, the idea of parental involvement has been a matter of interest to educators and parents for quite some time. The creation of the PTA dates back to the previous century and has been a catalyst for parental activities for generations. Room mothers, field-trip chaperones, library and clinic volunteers, and a host of other parent-filled positions have been a part of the school landscape for as long as anyone can remember.

Not surprisingly researchers have studied whether parental involvement makes any difference in a child's success or failure at school. Their findings are encouraging. When you get involved in your child's education, good things are more likely to happen, and bad things are more likely to be avoided. For example, researchers found that (1) high parental participation cuts in half the likelihood of a child ending up in the lower half of their class; (2) the likelihood of suspension from school is tripled when there is low involvement from parents; and (3) students with low parental involvement are two and a half times more likely to repeat a grade.[1]

All of these findings are important, but the first is remarkable. Think about it. If you get involved in the educational life of your child, your child is 50 percent less likely to end up in the bottom half of the class. If, as mentioned earlier, higher-achieving students receive better instruction from teachers, this is no small matter. Your faithful involvement in your child's education can have a powerful impact on your child's overall experience at school.

Another study revealed that higher levels of parental involvement resulted in better test scores in reading.[2] At the same time, teachers reported fewer learning problems. These results held true even after things like the child's IQ, ethnic background, and socioeconomic status were eliminated as possible explanations for success.

The importance of parental involvement seems to outweigh many other factors like how rich or poor a family might be or whether a family is an ethnic minority. Even the child's IQ, within reasonable limits, does not seem to matter. A study of parental involvement completed by researchers at the Stanford Center for the Study of Families revealed that "regardless of parents' level of income or education, a positive correlation existed between attendance of parents at events especially planned for them and their children's receiving higher grades."[3]

In a review of the research on parental involvement for her master's thesis, Vickie Lynne Luchuck compiled the following list of benefits for when Mom and/or Dad are involved in their children's public school education.

1. More positive attitude toward school
2. Higher achievement
3. Higher quality and more level-appropriate work
4. Completion of more homework in less time
5. Fewer students placed in special-education programs
6. Higher graduation rates, and greater enrollment in postsecondary education[4]

While we most frequently think of mothers in relation to school activities, a father's involvement is also important. Using information from a National Household Education Survey, Christine Winquist Nord determined that the father's involvement is just as likely to have a positive impact on a child's success in school as the mother's involvement.[5] Nord also found that with Dad's involvement children are more likely to get A's, to participate in extracurricular activities, and to enjoy school.

For all those divorced fathers out there who feel like their influence on their children has been reduced to weekend movies and occasional visits, the research is encouraging. Virtually the same results are found for nonresident fathers who are willing to make the extra effort to stay involved in their children's school experiences.[6]

If you are a parent, you are probably not surprised by any of this. This kind of research probably only confirms what you intuitively knew all along; children need quality time and attention, and when they get it, they are more likely to flourish. It seems so simple and obvious, doesn't it? Nevertheless, I offer these pieces of formalized study to encourage you to stay involved.

As a parent you can lapse into periods of complacency when there is no apparent crisis demanding your attention. This is easy to do. We get tired, and the pace of life can be frenetic. However, too many mothers and fathers have adopted a parenting style that is characterized primarily by crisis management. Unless a situation demands their attention, parents often fall into a sort of unintentional routine.

The kind of parental involvement I am urging is one of intentional, proactive activity that does not wait for a problem to emerge. Faith is what characterizes this kind of parental involvement because results are not automatic. Any farmer will tell you there is a good bit of plowing and weeding and watering and fertilizing before you see any growth. In the same way, parental involvement in your child's school experiences involves working now to yield a harvest later.

We live in an age of experts, sound-bite psychology, and three-step procedures for solving all of life's difficulties. Intuitively, though, we know that raising children is messy business. While no one knows your child better than you, at times you have probably wondered if you have taken the right approach with your child. My children are grown, and if I could do it all over again, I can think of several situations I would handle differently. However, I suspect that the vast majority of the time I would be just as unsure of myself now as I was as a young parent.

In retrospect, I can see that it has been God's gracious, sovereign work in my family's life that has redeemed my faltering efforts to parent. I hope the truth that God is deeply interested in your own family gives you the courage you need to press on in the parenting struggle.

Here's a quiz that will teach you something about being a good parent. Of the four choices below, which one do you think is most likely to produce better grades for your child in school?

A. Volunteering at school
B. Monitoring homework
C. Discussing school with your child
D. Communicating with your child's teacher

The encouraging news is that all of the above activities contribute to increased school success for children, but researchers Ho and Willms looked at these four choices and sought to determine whether any one of them impacted the success of eighth-grade students more than the others.[7] The one that stood out was letter C—talking with your child about school.

This is not to say the other choices did not matter. Indeed, they are all important ingredients to the working definition of parental involvement. Nevertheless, there seems to be something special about giving a child time to talk about school while at home. Ironically, this aspect of parental involvement can be both the simplest and the most difficult to achieve.

We've all seen a father or mother in the grocery store or some other public place interacting with his or her child in a way that makes us want to intervene. The continuous stream of negative comments makes you cringe. It's painful to watch. What is so blatantly obvious to an outsider is often a blind spot to the individual involved. What's the interaction like between you and your child? If you're like most people, you'll probably concede it isn't perfect, but overall it seems all right to you. Without encouraging you to labor under unnecessary guilt (parents absorb guilt like a sponge), may I simply encourage you to recommit your efforts to give your child the kind of patient, undistracted conversational time that you know will help him or her to flourish?

If someone were to videotape your interactions with your child over a period of several days and then play it back to you, what would it reveal? Would you see times of intentional and focused conversation? Or would you see only bits and pieces of conversation offered on the fly? An effective mother or father probably needs to be able to multitask—to do several things at once. Having a meaningful conversation with your child is not something to do while multitasking. It doesn't work between husband and wife, so why would it work between parent and child?

As you wrestle with whether to send your child to the local public school, I encourage you to do so with your eyes open and under the best prayerful counsel you can find. If you do decide to send your child to a public school, I would like to offer some ways to make the public school experience as positive as possible.

Visit your child's school. One writer has commented that "schools are generally closed societies, with an unspoken tradition of keeping parents at a distance."[8] It would be hard to know just how intentional that alleged unspoken tradition has been, but many parents do say they feel awkward going to their child's school. That is understandable, but I would encourage you to push past the awkwardness. The truth is that many schools are now actively looking for ways to encourage parental involvement.

As the "Goals 2000: Educate America Act" is enacted, each state is required to show how it is going to raise parental participation in schools.[9] A public school in Rochester, New York, reported having 297 parents show up on "Take Your Parents to School Day," and they stayed all day![10] Other schools have created special rooms in their buildings where parents can gather and cultivate a more vibrant relationship with their child's school.

Meet the principal or assistant principal if you can. Ask for a tour of the building. Get a feel for life in the halls and cafeteria and library. This is the world where your child spends the majority of his or her time. Try to get in touch with that world.

Get to know your child's teacher. There was a day when teachers made home visits. Though that may be a thing of the past, perhaps your child's teacher would respond to an invitation to dinner or to a light dessert later in the evening. This communicates so very much. Without a direct word on the matter, your child will recognize that his or her education is important to you. The teacher will get the message that you appreciate his or her efforts to teach your child.

Show up for scheduled conference opportunities even when things are going well. If you don't have anything to discuss, make the effort to show up and tell your child's teacher that you appreciate all the hard work. Find ways to keep the lines of communication open—an occasional telephone call or a written note. Even if the content of the communication is light, the larger message that you care enough to be involved is significant.

How does this translate in the classroom? Does the child feel a heightened connection with his or her teacher? Does the teacher feel a similar link or bond to the child? If we are influenced consciously or subconsciously by things as slight as name, height, eyeglasses, and so on, just think how much we're influenced by getting to know someone beyond outward appearance. Do not underestimate the power of simple interactions with your child's teacher.

Volunteer to help in your child's school. Even if you aren't a stay-at-home mom or dad, opportunities to volunteer are usually available if you are willing to make some sacrifices. There are a whole host of activities that may be available to you in your child's classroom, from reading to children to having a child (who is not necessarily your own) read to you to chaperoning a field trip. Consult with your child's teacher about the possibilities. Cultivating a trusting relationship with the teacher will go a long way toward making this consultation go well.

If opportunities are limited in your child's room, you may find volunteer opportunities in the school library, cafeteria, or even the school office. Though you may not be making direct contact with your child, you will be put in touch with your child's world of school. At the same time, the message of concern and commitment will be communicated in ways your child will not miss.

71

Visit your child on special occasions. Always extend the courtesy of talking with your child's teacher and any other appropriate school official ahead of time, but on occasion come to school and eat lunch with your child. If your child is giving a report in class or is participating in any sort of special school activity, be there. This would include events such as school plays, sporting events, fairs, and exhibits.

Keep your child's teacher informed. Each morning your child's teacher watches some thirty children file into class, each with his or her own story. Four of them are struggling with some sort of sickness, five did not get enough sleep last night, one has a dog about to have puppies at home, another is coping with the fact that his dog was hit by a car four days ago. Some might be dealing with family conflict, while another could be anticipating a joyous event like a birthday. These and many other factors impact children's moods as they move through a school day.

The teacher is much better able to respond to Johnny's defiant attitude if he or she has been made aware that there is a divorce unfolding on the home front, or that a grandmother is in the hospital, or that someone has been bullying him on the playground. Let the teacher know. Follow up with periodic conversations with the teacher regarding how he or she perceives the situation. This will not only keep you informed, but will help the teacher stay mindful of the situation.

It will come as no surprise to learn that communication is at the heart of parental involvement. As fundamental as that insight may seem, we all struggle with putting it into practice. Husbands and wives. Bosses and employees. Parents and children. Teachers and students. It takes work, and a willingness to wrestle with the disappointments and failures that can be a real part of trying to communicate with other humans. While I could offer you long lists of things you can do, there is an intangible dimension to this whole enterprise. You should not look for a parental involvement checklist, do everything on the list, and then use your checklist as a defense when things don't work out as promised. Try loving your husband or wife that way and you quickly learn how anemic the relationship becomes.

Attending PTA meetings, teacher conferences, school plays, and all the rest is a vital ingredient in parental involvement. However, you can faithfully attend PTA meetings and sit in the back disengaged, and then grumble later about how they do things. You can show up for the parent-teacher conference, move through the motions, and then conclude that the teacher seems a bit aloof. Oh well, you tried, didn't you? You can accompany your child on a field trip and then complain about how exhausting it was at that evening's dinner table. You get the idea. Attitude is important in life, and this matter of parental involvement in your child's school experience is no exception.

For any of these parental involvement activities to yield the fruit in your child's life that you desire, you must invest these activities, including your at-home conversations with your child, with enthusiasm, determination, and a sense of positive commitment. This is the powerful lubricant that makes it all work.

Give your child's teacher a break. Teachers are human just like you. When you walk into a parent-teacher conference in an adversarial state of mind, what kind of reaction do you think you are going to get? Teachers can sense when parents want to work together to make things better and when they just want to blame someone else besides themselves for their child's lack of success. They get tired. Teaching is an exhausting job, and it often extends well into the evening.

73

Much of the criticism leveled at the public schools is beyond the scope of a teacher's ability to correct, and yet the teachers are often the convenient lightning rod for that criticism. Try approaching your child's teacher with words of encouragement and affirmation. Build a relationship of trust. Understand that this teacher has twenty-nine other students who have a legitimate claim on his or her attention and energies; they have a story of their own.

Understand that we all react to particular personality types, and we each have our own preferences. Resist the temptation to lose enthusiasm if you don't find yourself clicking with your child's teacher on a personal level. Show yourself to be consistent and trustworthy, and you stand a far better chance of making your parental involvement translate into positive benefits for your child.

As you navigate these waters of parental involvement, you may be a bit unsure of yourself. Take heart; a number of resources are available to you. The national Parent Teacher Association (PTA) publishes a bimonthly magazine, *Our Children*. They make available other literature as well, like a fifteen-page guide called "A Leader's Guide to Parent and Family Involvement." Although various booklets may drift in and out of print, you can expect an organization like this to be a rich resource of ideas and encouragement for parental involvement.

With the Internet becoming more and more available to the average family, untold riches can be mined from your home computer. A recent bit of web surfing unearthed websites sponsored by the Pennsylvania PTA and the Wisconsin PTA, to name just a couple. Each site is a helpful source of ideas, literature, and encouragement for parental involvement, regardless of the state in which you live. I would encourage you to do your own Internet search, confident that you will find many useful resources.

6

How Did We Get Here?

As I have talked with colleagues in the secular as well as the Christian community, I've seen how polarizing the issue of school choice can be. People end up drawing lines in the sand in us-against-them militancy, which is unfortunate. You may encounter some of this as you wrestle with the schooling choice that is best for your child. Advice comes from many different sources—friends and family, church and civic groups, television exposés, magazine and journal articles, and books such as this one. You may find yourself pulled in several directions at once, as one impassioned friend expresses a view contrary to that of another friend. Each friend speaks with such conviction, while you grow more and more uncertain. This chapter will help.

If you have no idea how any of this educational business got started or how it all fits together, you are much more likely to be pushed and pulled from one sound bite to another. To help you sort through the sometimes shrill voices and militant posturing, I want to offer you a perspective that takes into account the history of the choices before you. Some of this may surprise you. For example, while some would have you believe public schools have always been the choice of Americans, in truth private and home schools have been around far longer than our public schools. But I'm getting ahead of myself. Let's back up a bit, and take a more organized look at how public, private, and home schools have found their way onto the educational landscape in America.

To begin our thumbnail sketch of the history of education here in America, we must imagine life in the original colonies. No telephones or microwaves or interstates or railroads or lightbulbs or automobiles or computers. No penicillin or Band-Aids or blood-pressure devices or Novocain or tetanus shots. Life was hard, and as you might expect people spent a great deal of effort just surviving. The work day was long, leaving little time for free-time pursuits such as learning to read. Because schools did not exist, parents taught their children as time would allow.

Home schooling, then, was the necessary norm during America's early days, and it has enjoyed an uninterrupted existence to the present. Many think home schooling is a new phenomenon resulting from dissatisfaction with the public schools, but the majority of Americans home schooled for hundreds of years before the emergence of public schools. Certainly public schools have had an impact on home schooling, but home schooling itself is anything but new.

Private schools have been around almost as long. As rough settlements gave way to towns, and life eased ever so slightly, parental concern for education occasionally gave way to the formation of some sort of local schooling option. These were not public schools as we would understand that term today, however. Where schools did exist, they were private schools that charged tuition. Sending your child to school would have been a luxury reserved for those with financial resources.

In some cases, this education would take the form of an apprenticeship, which might include an expectation that the child would be taught to read and write. At other times it would take the form of a tutor, in either a one-on-one or small-group setting. In all cases the parents paid for the service. Free public education for America's children simply did not exist for hundreds of years.

Home schooling and private schools are not the strange, radical alternatives that some would have you believe they are. When you consider centuries of American history in which the norm for parents was either home schooling, or, for the resourceful minority, private schools, you begin to wonder how we arrived at such a vast and complex machine as the modern public education system in America. You also might wonder, given America's deep roots in home schooling and private schools, how it is that nowadays public schooling often seems to have an adversarial relationship with these other forms of schooling. The answers to these and other important questions can be found in the fascinating story of how public schools came into existence in the first place.

The first law that had to do with education was passed in Massachusetts in 1642. Growing out of a concern that not all parents were making sure their children learned to read and write, this law mandated under penalty of fine that every parent see to the education of their child. The state of Massachusetts sent representatives to people's homes to make sure the law was being obeyed. While people often cite this as the first law that insisted on public and universal education, it made no provision for schools or teachers, and females were not acceptable students.[1] The state simply wanted to make parents do their educational duty. There were no schools, no taxes, no teachers, no curriculum.

As might be expected, trying to enforce this law was nearly impossible, and five years later the state gave it another legal try with the passage of the famous Old Deluder Satan Law. Recognizing that it is not enough to insist that parents educate their children, the state tried to put more teeth into their legal mandate by requiring towns to pay someone to be accountable for the education of the children.

On November 11, 1647, Massachusetts passed a law requiring any town with over fifty households to appoint and pay a teacher. If the town was over a hundred households, they were expected to establish a grammar school. This was known as the Old Deluder Satan Law because it included this statement: "It being one chief project of that old deluder, Satan, to keep men from the knowledge of the Scriptures . . . that learning may not be buried in the grave of our fathers in the church and commonwealth, the Lord assisting our endeavors. . . ."[2] Thus, a part of the impulse that drove the state to educate its children was to ensure their ability to read and understand the Bible.

Note again that the state made no provision to pay for any of this educational effort. No taxes. No school buildings. No curriculum guidelines. No assistance with teacher salaries. The state simply wanted parents to educate their children, and they were ready to fine communities that did not comply.

Imagine this historical narrative is a video and let's fast-forward to 1791. In this year there were still no public schools as we know them today, but the tenth amendment to the Bill of Rights was ratified, which gave states the right to provide and govern public educational practice. Even though we have jumped ahead in our narrative by more than a hundred years, I should tell you there was a lot of spirited political debate that led to this significant event. While it is beyond the scope of this book to give a detailed treatment of all the debate, I will explain some of the basics.

Americans have various opinions about how much the government should be allowed to regulate its citizens' activities. Most of us would concede certain areas of authority to the government without much objection—traffic regulations, basic business practices that protect us from being swindled, the building of bridges and highways. There are many areas of life, however, that some feel the government has little or no business regulating. The right to bear arms is an increasingly provocative topic, the discussion often centering on where the government's authority begins and ends. Others might complain about the building permits and inspections required for improving one's home.

Depending on the issue, it is not uncommon for Americans to feel like the State has moved from helpful regulation to meddling. In many ways the history of education in America is a history of this regulating vs. meddling debate. The idea of having to pay taxes to educate someone else's child, for example, was hotly contested. Historian Lawrence Cremin writes, "The fight for free schools was a bitter one and for twenty-five years the outcome was uncertain. . . . Legislation passed one year was sometimes repealed the next."[3] Another historian characterized the struggle for tax-supported public education, in terms of its emotional intensity, as second only to the abolition of slavery.[4]

That it took an amendment to the Bill of Rights in 1791 to declare that the State did indeed have the right to mandate public educational practice indicates just how serious and volatile this issue was. It's tempting to muse, "If you think you had problems back then, you ought to hear the debate today!" Keeping in mind this issue of how much authority the government should have over the education of its citizens' children, let's press the fast-forward button again and move to the middle of the next century.

By 1850 cities like New York and Boston were well established, but the Midwest and West were still being settled. Bear in mind this was only about 150 years from the present, and still there were no public schools, even though the state had established its legal right to regulate such matters decades earlier. Where schools existed, they were strictly private in nature, with the price of tuition determining who would attend. For example, in 1850 there were 138 private schools in New York City, and in Massachusetts there was some 350 tuition-based schools.[5] This was all about to change, however, as America embraced the industrial revolution.

The eastern part of the United States was more established at this point, so it's not surprising Massachusetts passed the very first compulsory-attendance law. This occurred in 1852, approximately eight years prior to the start of the American Civil War. In 1867, two years after the end of the war, Vermont became the second state to pass a compulsory-attendance law, and around this time the public school movement was born.

While some might resist the degree to which the government regulates the freedom we have in educating our children, it is worth noting that the government succeeded in framing the debate with the first compulsory-attendance law back in 1852. The question now is not whether you may choose to neglect your child's education, but which methods of education are acceptable.

There are a number of reasons public schools came into being, some of which are more political than pedagogical. One event that gave great energy to the government's view that public schools were necessary was the tremendous influx of immigrants during the last half of the nineteenth century.

In our present state as a developed country, it is difficult for most of us to imagine what this immigration was like. Historian Lawrence Cremin observed that "some forty million people entered the country between 1876 and 1980, constituting one of the largest migrations in history."[6] The vast majority of these people were not prepared to participate in American culture. By the 1920s a third of America's population was either immigrants or children of immigrants.[7]

Language was a major issue, and it is no wonder Russians and Germans and Poles and Hungarians gravitated to their own little communities within cities like New York and Boston. Not surprisingly, the government wondered how this mass of humanity would ever become contributing members to the American enterprise. One of the ways our government dealt with such a diversity of people was by instituting public schools. Let me illustrate.

I have had the privilege of traveling overseas in recent years, and sometimes the language barriers make going to a restaurant quite a challenge. Occasionally I was tired or hurried, so I looked for a way to avoid the difficulty of making myself understood in a restaurant. The answer? McDonald's. Yes, I confess I have eaten a McDonald's hamburger in Paris, Moscow, and Vienna. You might wonder how an Austrian cheeseburger or a Russian order of french fries tastes. They're all the same. You could close your eyes as you bite into a Russian McDonald's cheeseburger and easily imagine that you were in Orlando, Florida, or Des Moines, Iowa.

We have much in our culture that has made our daily experience rather uniform. We can enter a K-Mart in Tacoma, Washington, or Richmond, Virginia, and we all know what a blue-light special is about. I can buy a widget at the Sears store in Topeka, Kansas, and return it to a Sears store in Lansing, Michigan. I can watch the evening news on NBC, CBS, ABC, or CNN from anywhere in the country and see the exact same broadcast as anyone else in the U.S. We all respond to the same hit movies, sports stars, and television soap operas. These and many other shared experiences shape our common experience and contribute to our understanding of what it means to be American.

Our public school experience is much the same way. The government launched an intentional strategy for converting throngs of immigrants to the American way of life. As one observer put it, "Universal public education was the means by which individual liberty and a democratic state would be guaranteed."[8] While there is certainly diversity among our nation's public schools, there are also a lot of commonalities. They include the pledge of allegiance (with so many immigrants, you can understand why the government thought it was important for people to pledge allegiance to the flag), pep rallies, washing chalkboards at the end of the day, recess, homeroom, Valentine's Day parties, fire drills, lunch money, number-two pencils, dress codes, photo days, yearbooks, and the list goes on.

An educated citizenry meant more than a people who could multiply fractions or read want ads. It also meant a people completely acculturated to the norms and values of the dominant culture. This works as long as there is widespread agreement on what the norms and values ought to be. But as soon as people begin to disagree with the norms and values being imposed, government is perceived to be meddling.

A second factor that gave energy to the public school movement was the emergence of child labor laws. Life in rural America was typically characterized by long days of labor that included children working alongside their parents in order to survive. In fact, the tradition of taking summers off from school came from the need of families to have every member home during harvest season.

However, in the industrialized east, the situation wasn't much different. The absence of child labor laws created an environment in which it was not uncommon for young children to hold down full-time jobs. Based on the 1900 census, 1.75 million or 18.2 percent of the nation's children between the ages of 10 and 15 were working full-time jobs.[9] Because census takers recorded only those children with full-time jobs, researchers assume many more children were working part-time hours. It's fair to say many children did not receive anything resembling a basic education because they were expected to work.

If an educated citizenry was necessary for the best interests of America, it appeared many parents were not holding up their moral and civil obligations in this matter. While it is probably not fair to say the State created public schools and compulsory-attendance laws to get rid of what they considered to be child labor abuses, the two worked together in a complementary fashion. For example, in 1903 Florence Kelley declared, "The best child labor law is a compulsory-education law covering forty weeks of the year and requiring the consecutive attendance of all the children to the age of fourteen years."[10]

As might be expected, not everyone embraced these legally mandated changes. Some families resisted because they felt they had the right to determine the educational destiny of their children and did not appreciate the government's interference. Others were likely moved to resistance because they felt they needed the income generated by their children. Some resisted because of religious convictions. Catholics, for example, detected an unhealthy Protestant influence in the newly formed public schools.

While large numbers quietly complied with the new laws, government officials believed the resistance was enough to warrant employment of full-time truancy officers, who kept quite busy. It would take decades before America's youth were participating in public education as they are today. For example, as late as 1913 one-half of children in America attending school received their education in a one-room school.[11] Secondary school development came later. In 1890 only 5.6 percent of those eligible even entered high school. By 1930, the number was barely above 50 percent, and only 29 percent were graduating.[12]

From our present perspective, it may seem like public education in America has always been the widely accepted, well-developed system that we see today. It was not that long ago, however, that the lack of a high school diploma was more the norm than the exception.

As early as 1923, a challenge to compulsory attendance in public schools found its way from Nebraska to the United States Supreme Court.[13] In essence, the Court ruled that the government's right to regulate educational practice was not absolute; parents retained certain rights that were beyond the reach of government. Two years later another Supreme Court ruling struck down a strict interpretation of the compulsory-attendance law in Oregon. The majority decision stated, "The child is not the mere creature of the state; those who nurture him and direct his destiny have the right and high duty, to recognize and prepare him for additional obligations."[14] These two early Supreme Court rulings are examples of the struggle between citizen-parents and the government to define the boundary between regulating and meddling.

Private schooling, which had long been a part of the educational landscape, continued to exist, and without a great deal of resistance came to be a legally acceptable alternative to public schooling. On the other hand, home schooling, which had been the norm for so long, had been all but legislated out of existence. This was a legal right that parents were going to have to win back through the same courts that had taken it away.

In 1950 a home schooling couple from Illinois was convicted of violating the public-or-private compulsory-attendance law.[15] Appealing to that state's Supreme Court, the couple prevailed in having the original conviction overturned. The court stated, "The number of persons being taught does not determine whether a place is a school." Additionally, the court explained, "Compulsory education laws are enacted to enforce the natural obligations of parents to provide an education for their young, an obligation which corresponds to the parents' right of control over the child." In 1987 the Massachusetts Supreme Court ruled in favor of a home schooling family stating that the object of compulsory education laws is "that all children shall be educated, not that they shall be educated in any particular way."[16]

In 1967 a home schooling family in New Jersey was fined $2,490 by a local magistrate for noncompliance of the state's compulsory-attendance laws.[17] The New Jersey Supreme Court overturned the decision, stating that the defendant's home instruction met the standards of public school equivalency. Many other cases were brought before local and state courts, and gradually the legal right of parents to choose private schools or home schooling was wrestled back from the government.

When yet another case reached the U.S. Supreme Court in 1972, this time involving the right of the Amish to opt out of public schooling, Justice Burger wrote, "This primary role of the parents in the upbringing of their children is now established beyond debate as an enduring tradition."[18]

These and many other cases together form a kind of legal mosaic that has helped to enforce the government's right to regulate public educational policy while preserving parents' right to meet governmental requirements by alternative methods.

As of 1998, thirty-five states had passed specific laws preserving the right of parents to educate their children at home, while the remaining states make qualified provision for it in one form or another.

In 1983 Michael Farris, an attorney and ordained minister, founded the Home School Legal Defense Association (HSLDA). The impact of the HSLDA on home schooling in America is incalculable. Available to every home schooler in the country for a yearly fee of a hundred dollars, this organization provides legal counsel and defense as needed. In 1990–91, for example, the HSLDA handled nearly two thousand cases across the country.[19]

While landmark cases have preserved the fundamental right of parents to make educational choices on behalf of their children, these did not come without great effort. Whether your resistance to public schools is based on religious conviction or academic concerns, your right as a parent to consider alternatives to the public schools is the result of more than a century of political and legal struggles. And the battle is not over. The government continues to argue for its right to regulate or meddle, depending on how you look at it.

Resistance to public schooling has existed from the earliest days of its development. Home schooling and private schools existed long before the first compulsory-attendance law and have continued uninterrupted to the present day, despite that it became necessary to fight for the parental right to choose.

Understanding the historical context of public schools, private schools, and home schooling in America should liberate you as a parent to resist those who would dismiss alternatives to the status quo as being too radical or unprecedented.

Caveat Emptor

The Private/Christian School Option

Private schooling has a long history in America and predates the formation of public schools by several hundred years. If you find yourself considering the move to a private school, you can take comfort in knowing you are not alone in your deliberations. In 1993–94 private schools accounted for nearly 25 percent of all schools in the nation and 10.7 percent of its students.[1] Additionally, these private schools represent a wide range of affiliations. For example, approximately 30 percent of non-Catholic schools in the country during this same time period were Seventh Day Adventist, Missouri Synod Lutheran, Episcopalian, or Hebrew Day or other Jewish schools. Educator Joseph Newman points out, "Throughout the twentieth century, private schools have enrolled between 7 and 14 percent of the nation's elementary and secondary students."[2]

During the 1995–96 school year, Chicago had 387 private schools compared to 550 public schools.[3] Not only did one student in five attend a private school in Chicago, but 36 percent of its public school teachers sent their children to private schools. As of 2001, the Association of Christian Schools International reported more than five thousand member schools in ninety countries, with a combined student enrollment of some 1,030,000.[4] Private schools do indeed represent a viable and ongoing alternative to public schools.

Enrolling your child in a private school has a number of consequences, not only for your child, but for your entire family. If you have been thinking about this option, one of the first considerations to emerge probably has been the financial cost. For most parents this is a big issue for which sacrifices will have to be made. For some it may mean less ambitious vacation or recreational activities, and for others it may mean a second job for both Mom and Dad. Nevertheless, parents make this sacrificial choice in favor of private schooling all across the country.

The reason private schools require a financial sacrifice is, of course, because all parents are required by law to pay taxes in support of the public schools. But what if parents could choose to use their tax dollars to pay for private school tuition? The idea of the government providing financial vouchers to parents for just such a purpose is being explored in several parts of the country. While not yet available to the public at large, this is an idea that may eventually result in financial relief for those considering the private school option. For that reason, let's pause to see just where the voucher movement stands at this moment.

The idea of the government providing a financial voucher to be used by the parent for any school option of their choice is one of the most controversial and politically contested issues on the American education landscape. The oldest voucher program in the country is in Milwaukee and has been in place since around 1989.[5] This program, as well as the voucher programs in Cleveland, Ohio, and the states of Michigan and Florida are currently receiving a good bit of scrutiny.

As might be expected, opponents of the idea express concerns over using public money to fund students who may end up at religious schools. Along with the issue of separation between church and state, another argument against vouchers is that money used for vouchers is essentially money lost to the local school system. Advocates of a voucher system build their case on the idea that public schools have tragically failed our children, necessitating a rescue of the most dramatic variety. The debate can be intense.

In a *USA Today* article, authors Henry and DeBarros state, "In the national debate over these programs, most arguments center on whether vouchers are passports out of failing inner-city schools, windfalls for church coffers, violations of church-state divisions or death knells to public education. Ultimately however, the central issue is money."[6] In the summer of 1996, The American Federation of Teachers brought suit against the voucher program in Cleveland.[7] The legal battles continue in virtually every location where voucher programs exist.

At present, voucher systems target the most needy situations rather than offering a universal option to the general public school population. For example, the Florida voucher system is statewide, but as of October 2000 it had reached only fifty-one students because the program is extended only to those students attending a school that had deemed to be failing two years in a row.[8] Likewise, Michigan offers vouchers only to students in districts that are failing.[9] To qualify for a voucher in Milwaukee, your income must be no more than 1.75 times the federal poverty level.[10]

Because vouchers are still relatively new and have been tried in only a few locations nationwide, it is too early to predict their future. The National Education Association, which opposes the idea of vouchers, offers, "In general, evaluations of voucher students' achievement show no or only small improvements relative to comparable public school students."[11] However, a recent study of the voucher programs in three cities indicated that the African-American students that had been in the voucher program for two years showed they had outperformed their public school peers.[12] In truth, there is simply too little real data in these formative years for voucher programs to draw any meaningful conclusions about the academic virtues of voucher use.

In the meantime, highly politicized legal action continues to unfold in various courts, making the future of vouchers tenuous and unpredictable. If you find yourself facing the real opportunity to avail yourself of a voucher program, the word of encouragement is the same for any option presented in this book. Do your homework and stay engaged before, during, and after your decision to participate.

Parents who choose to enroll their students in private schools without the financial benefit of a voucher often make certain assumptions about what they are getting for their money. For example, they might be attracted to smaller class sizes, more personal attention, a better attitude among teachers as well as fellow students, a value system or worldview more consistent with their own beliefs, and a host of benefits in the area of personal safety. These are among the benefits people most frequently cite in support of private schools. Many parents are willing to make sacrifices to buy these and other perceived benefits for their child.

Given all that is at stake here, it would not only be reasonable but responsible for parents to ask whether they would be getting their money's worth. Let's take a closer look at what you should and shouldn't expect from private schools.

In an earlier chapter I referred to the amount of wasted time in a typical public school classroom because of the sheer number of students the teacher must manage. Getting thirty students to move through the day can be time consuming. While it is not uncommon to find private schools with smaller class sizes than in public schools, parents shouldn't assume this is the case unilaterally.

Undoubtedly some public school classrooms in America have a tragically large number of students. As a whole, however, there is not much difference between the public and private sector when it comes to class size. As a quick example, in the 1993–94 school year, the average class size for Christian schools that were members of the Association of Christian Schools International (ACSI) was 20.0.[13] Among those schools that were members of another accrediting association, Christian Schools International (CSI), the number was 20.5.[14] The national average for public schools during that same year? It may come as a surprise that the public school figure was only 23.8—a difference, on average, of only four students per classroom.[15] Obviously the numbers are going to vary from location to location, and in your own specific situation you may find local private schools with class sizes significantly smaller than in public schools in your area.

This brings up a separate issue. Even if your local private school is offering a class size of fifteen, how good should that make you feel? Logic would suggest smaller class sizes go a long way toward solving the problem of wasted time. This logic has not escaped the notice of public school educators. Former U.S. vice president Al Gore announced that the government would spend over one billion dollars in one fiscal year (1999–2000) on the

Class Size Reduction Initiative.[16] You read the figure correctly—over one billion dollars. This spending initiative grew out of significant research on the impact that class size has on student achievement.

In the most noted study to date, Tennessee's Project STAR (Student-Teacher Achievement Ratio) examined kindergarten through third-grade classrooms across the state.[17] Covering a four-year period and 7,500 students, some students were placed in small classes (thirteen to seventeen students), some in regular classes (twenty-two to twenty-six), and still others in a regular classroom (twenty-two to twenty-six) but with a full-time teacher aide. Teachers did not receive any special training, and teachers with aides could use the additional help any way they wished. As researchers collected data on achievement, motivation, and self concept, they came to four general conclusions:

1. There were positive results in small classes, irregardless of grade, school size, or location of school.
2. The positive results were there for boys as well as girls.
3. Inner-city and minority students especially benefited from small classes.
4. Results for students in small classes lasted through grade seven and beyond even though students were placed back into regular classrooms at grade four. For example, when these same students were evaluated years later (most were in the tenth grade), researchers reported, "Pupils who had been in small classes were rated as expending more effort in the classroom, taking greater initiative with regard to learning activities, and displaying less disruptive or inattentive behavior compared to their peers who had been in regular-size classes."[18]

All of this would seem to support the benefits of reduced class size. However, few things in life are as straightforward as we wish they were, and class size is no exception. Logistically, public schools must wrestle with staffing issues, even if the money is there. For example, during the 1996–97 school year, California spent $1.5 billion to reduce class size and found it enormously difficult to find certified teachers to fill the new slots.[19]

Even more distressing were the mixed signals that came from later research. During the mid-1980s the state of Indiana sponsored research similar to the Tennessee study. Among its findings was this statement: "The results for academic achievement were mixed—at times, small classes were found to have superior outcomes and, at times, the large classes performed better."[20]

In East Austin, Texas, the school district allocated several hundred thousand dollars each year to reduce class size over a several-year period.[21] Despite the effort, student achievement and attendance remained low in several of the schools. In two of the schools that showed improvement, it was discovered that the primary effort was concentrated on raising student achievement instead of trying to reduce class size. Thus, even though originally we might have thought of this as merely a numbers problem, it appears the situation is more complicated than that.

In an examination of over one hundred studies on class size, one researcher noted, "Research does not support the expectation that smaller classes will of themselves result in greater academic gains for students. The effects of class size on student learning varies [*sic*] by grade level, pupil characteristics, subject areas, teaching methods, and other learning interventions."[22]

While not denying the likely benefits of reducing class size, it is important to note that it is not necessarily a straight line from smaller numbers of students to the desired benefits. If time is lost trying to manage a classroom of thirty students, it does not naturally follow that reducing the class to twelve or fifteen students will automatically eliminate lost time or even cut it in half. Furthermore, if teachers simply conduct business as usual but with fewer students, at least some of the research tells us the advantage to your child would likely be nominal at best. In this we see further evidence that teaching at its core is a complex experience tied directly to the nature and quality of the human interaction that takes place.

Small numbers can help but only if the teacher works the situation to its best advantage. In other words, just because your child is heading off to a private school classroom with a dozen students does not automatically mean that he is better off than his public school counterpart.

Of course class size is only one item on a long list of possible advantages to the private school environment. Other issues include drug use, peers with a more wholesome outlook, student misbehavior, and personal safety and well-being. How certain can parents be that these advantages exist in private schools? The answer is somewhat elusive because the amount of conclusive research is not extensive. However, we can probably gain some insight from the research that is available.

A national, longitudinal study of eighth-graders sponsored by the U.S. Department of Education provided Steven Vryhof, a graduate student at the University of Chicago, with valuable information with which to compare students in member schools of Christian Schools International with their public school counterparts.[23] Just how different are Christian schools from public schools? When you're writing out a tuition check, how different is different enough?

Public schools exist to serve every child in the country, regardless of parental involvement or socioeconomic status, so one would expect the private/Christian school population to have a decided advantage in many of these areas under question. Without underachieving inner-city students and many students whose parents are uninvolved, it is not unreasonable to think the private/Christian school population would enjoy a distinctly different and more positive school experience than their public school counterparts. All of this makes Vryhof's findings particularly interesting.

Consider the issue of peer pressure or peer influence or the incidence of drug use or cigarette smoking. What about stealing in school or being threatened by another student? What about aspirations to go to college? All of these issues, and more, create an atmosphere at any school that communicates quiet but powerful messages about values and attitudes and how life should be viewed. Let's take a look at some of these categories and see how the private/Christian school population compares to that of the public school. Each figure in the following tables is a percentage of eighth-graders who were surveyed.

Number of cigarettes smoked per day

	Christian school student	Public school national average
I don't smoke	96.7	93.3
1/2 to 2 packs	.3	.8

Someone offered to sell students drugs

	Christian school student	Public school national average
Never	96.9	90.0
Once or twice	2.2	6.9

Someone threatened to hurt the student

	Christian school student	Public school national average
Never	80.5	72.2
Once or twice	15.3	21.3

Student had something stolen at school

	Christian school student	Public school national average
Never	61.6	50.9
Once or twice	32.7	40.9

As parents look for acceptable alternatives to a public school environment that they feel is unsafe or unwholesome, it is vitally important to realize Christian schools are not necessarily the safe haven some claim they are. In all of the above comparisons, the Christian school environment seems to be an improvement over the public school alternative. But just how big is the Christian school advantage when you consider the public school national average necessarily includes the worst of the worst pushing its numbers in a negative direction? Even without taking this into account, it is reasonable for parents to ask whether the differences are big enough to warrant the sacrifice each time they write out a tuition check. Of course these are only statistical averages. The differences may be more compelling in your specific situation.

What about some of the less dramatic but arguably just as important issues such as homework, life goals, getting along with teachers, or boredom? Consider these comparisons from the same Vryhof study.

How far in school do you think you will get?

	Christian school student	Public school national average
Will attend college	14.0	13.1

Number of hours spent on homework per week

	Christian school student	Public school national average
2 to 3 hours	25.0	24.2
3 to 5 1/2 hours	28.2	33.3
5 1/2 to 10 1/2 hours	22.1	18.8

Students get along well with teachers

	Christian school student	Public school national average
Agree	64.2	59.3
Disagree	20.3	27.1

Ever feel bored at school

	Christian school student	Public school national average
Once in a while	47.0	49.0
About half the time	28.3	24.9
Most of the time	22.8	22.2

Once again the private/Christian school tends to fare slightly better in most categories, but these statistics may not reveal the striking difference you had expected. This information is a snapshot of the students' perspective. What kind of picture do we get from those who teach in Christian schools?

A survey covering five years and over 430 Christian school teachers produced the following partial list of teacher concerns.[24] Are there any on the list that surprise you?

1. Inconsistent standards between home and school
2. Low spiritual level in homes
3. Lack of spiritual leadership among pupils
4. Little spiritual growth of students
5. Inadequate salary
6. Faculty frustration (for whatever reason)

A different survey produced the following partial list of Christian school teacher concerns:[25]

1. Discipline problems
2. Unmotivated students
3. Excessive teaching/student load
4. Lack of parental support for teachers
5. Parental disinterest in children's progress
6. Problems with the administration

Finally, consider the results of a survey of Christian school teachers across the country who were members of the American Association of Christian Schools.[26]

1. Teacher salaries
2. High teacher turnover; untrained administrators
3. General spiritual problems
4. Poor parental supervision of kids
5. Student spiritual problems
6. Parent spiritual problems (i.e., poor parental attitudes, dysfunctional families)
7. Teacher spiritual problems
8. Diminished commitment to Christian education
9. Government interference
10. Unqualified teachers/lack of preparation

These three surveys represent diverse samples of Christian school teachers over a course of several years, but there are some recurring themes. Less-than-exemplary student attitudes and a lack of positive parental involvement are concerns shared by teachers from all three surveys. This is a curious finding that warrants additional comment.

Parents leaning toward private/Christian schools often have certain hopes and assumptions that attract their attention. Depending on background and experience, these assumptions can vary. Nevertheless, parents often anticipate the private/Christian school environment to be one with good kids from good families being nurtured by good teachers in good ways. These assumptions are what make it possible for many parents to write out a tuition check.

It would be encouraging, for example, to know that your child is going to be sitting in classrooms with children similar to your own—coming from homes with involved parents sharing the same levels of Christian maturity. It would be a relief to know that all the students embraced the same set of Christian values and spiritual beliefs, and that they matched yours. It would also be a relief to know that all the teachers shared these

Christian values and beliefs. It would be comforting to think that teacher-administration conflict would be non-existent, since this is a staff committed to a nobler cause. As the surveys suggest, these assumptions are not valid.

Every Christian school has its own admission policy. Some are open to any student whose parents can afford the tuition. Others limit enrollment to children whose parents are members of a particular church. Some require at least one of the parents to give a credible declaration of his or her spiritual beliefs that is consistent with the school's stated beliefs. Some are broadly inclusive while others may be quite selective. However, even among schools with more restrictive admissions criteria, there is no guarantee that the children enrolled embrace the Christian beliefs of their parents. Some do, of course, but you would be misguided to think the Christian school environment is filled with committed Christian students. For example, when one Christian school administrator was queried, "deep concern was expressed about the growing secularism and materialism and anti-religious attitudes among the students in our Christian schools."[27]

You would be just as misguided to think all professing Christian parents shared the same convictions about child raising, the role of the school or teachers, appropriate classroom discipline, what constitutes reasonable homework, acceptable dress codes, and a host of other issues. Teachers and administrators will have their own personal convictions about these various matters. Frustrations and disappointments make the Christian school option less than the idyllic haven we all wish it were.

The spiritual dimension of your child's education may be the primary reason you opt for the Christian school alternative to public schools. If so, I'd like to alert you to an additional warning. The surveys above hint at the possibility that simply being in a Christian environment staffed by well-intentioned Christian teachers does not necessarily produce the desired result. In fact, some Christian teachers and administrators fear that this environment may sometimes be counterproductive in this area.

There's a saying that goes, "Familiarity breeds contempt." In an environment where prayer begins classes, students go to chapel two or three times a week, the Bible is part of the curriculum, students are required to memorize Scripture, and a part of the classroom discussion often includes how the topic at hand relates to a Christian perspective, some fear the sheer volume of exposure to Christian teaching desensitizes students. That which is holy and should elicit a sense of awe and wonder becomes common, ordinary, and tedious as a result of continuous exposure. If all you want is for your child to learn about the Bible, this concern is of small consequence to you. However, if you are hoping your child will develop a vibrant, transforming faith, you should read the following comments from Christian school administrators:

> Christian schools are in danger of teaching their students to pay lip service to the Lord.[28]

> Classroom devotions sometimes become an opportunity for reinforcing a teacher's control.[29]

> A widespread cynicism infects the student body—a cynicism that focuses on legalistic interpretation of regulations rather than their spiritual intent.[30] . . . We need wonder no longer why so few of our Christian high school graduates elect to serve the Lord in a full-time ministry as pastors, missionaries, church workers, and the like.[31]

> I get upset by the deadening mental passivity and docility of most of them, by minds that show the dangerous

signs of prolonged indoctrination and isolation that can only result in intellectual stagnation. I get upset by the parental and community pressures to turn out a safe product that preferably doesn't think too much, questions less, and generally gives offense to nothing and are one in thought, word, and dress.[32]

What are we to make of all this? Should we throw up our hands and conclude there is no worthwhile difference between private/Christian and public schools? That's not my intention. In spite of my criticism, I believe families can reap substantive benefits from private/Christian schools. It's worth noting that despite the comments of teachers and administrators in private/Christian schools, they nevertheless continue their efforts. Becoming aware of the realities of private/Christian schools should not necessarily drive you away from them. Instead, it should remind you that you cannot become any less vigilant in the life of your child just because you think you have purchased an improved version of school.

In the end, your responsibilities as a parent are not reduced in the slightest because you have sent your child to a private/Christian school. As a public school teacher, I often lamented what seemed to be the all-too-common practice of parents dropping their child at the school door and driving away as if they had fulfilled their responsibility for educating their child. Private school teachers, even in the most evangelical Christian environments, struggle with the same thing. The presence of chapel messages, memory verses, frequent prayer, small classrooms, and committed Christian teachers may pose a peculiar temptation to parents to relax a bit in the diligent oversight of their child's education, especially if they already feel they are going above and beyond the call of duty by sending their child to such a school.

Students get bored in private/Christian schools just like they do in public schools. At roughly the same rate, some have difficulty with their teachers, are threatened by peers at school, and deal with drug and cigarette issues. Please do not misunderstand these comments. I am not trying to convince you that there are no real benefits to sending your child to a private/Christian school, even in the categories I just listed. However, you should not be lulled into thinking that you can somehow scale back your level of attention and involvement because your tuition money has purchased an escape from all such problems. Of course, each situation is unique. You may think your local public school is so unacceptable and your local Christian school so excellent that the surveys in this chapter don't come anywhere close to representing your particular case. You may be right.

Behind all the administrators' comments and the surveys of Christian school teachers and students, hundreds of parents like you wrestled with whether to send their children to private/Christian schools. Did they know about the less-than-ideal world to which they were sending their child? Perhaps. Or perhaps they made assumptions that they shouldn't have. I simply want to encourage you as a parent to remain as involved and as vigilant as ever, even if you have significantly improved your child's educational experience by sending him or her to a private/Christian school.

Whether it is public or private/Christian schooling, the level of parental involvement seems to be the wild card in all of this. Anytime you make assumptions, whether in the academic or spiritual realm, that decrease your involvement as a parent, you increase the risk to your child.

I know of public schools in this country where Bible instruction is still part of the official curriculum. I know of Christian schools that quite frankly are so ineffective and spiritually misguided that I would have an easier time undoing the negative impact of a public school than of the Christian school. The important thing to remember is that you as a parent should never surrender your responsibility to make the most informed decision possible and to stay closely attuned to the consequences of your decision.

The Home Schooling
Option

How are you at riddles? See if you can answer the following question. What do C. S. Lewis and Winston Churchill have in common? Yes, both are from England, but the correct answer is more specific than that. Let me give you a clue. They share this in common with Abraham Lincoln and Thomas Edison. Need another clue? Alright, they all share this single feature in common with Albert Einstein, Mark Twain, Leo Tolstoy, George Patton, Wilbur Wright, Agatha Christie, Franklin Roosevelt, and Wolfgang Mozart. By now you may have figured out that all of these people have been home schooled.

I could have included others in this list, such as Daniel Webster, John Wesley, Albert Schweitzer, Blaise Pascal, Stonewall Jackson, Noel Coward, Charlie Chaplin, Alexander Graham Bell, and Claude Monet. They all received an education characterized by some combination of home schooling and private tutoring.

Of course, listing names of famous people does not prove that one form of schooling is superior to another.

105

It would not be difficult to produce an equally impressive list of people who were products of America's public schools. Gifted people often flourish in spite of circumstances, not because of them. Nevertheless, for those who view home schooling as a gross disservice to children, it may come as a surprise that some seem to do quite well outside the mainstream experience of the traditional classroom.

In the early 1970s, an estimated ten to fifteen thousand home schoolers were scattered across America.[1] At the beginning of the new millennium, those estimates ran as high as 1.5 million.[2] The practice of educating children at home has changed from a relatively unknown, sometimes clandestine activity to something of a cultural movement.

The latter half of the twentieth century saw the development of a burgeoning industry of support for those who opted to home school, and it continues to thrive. Curriculum materials geared to the home school population are widely available, and well-organized support groups are easy to find for all but the most isolated home educators. Many of these parents get together for field trips, spelling and geography bees, and a host of extracurricular activities. Home school leader Michael Farris is a key figure behind plans to open a college in Virginia that caters specifically to home schooled students.[3]

Despite this impressive growth, people continue to ask questions about this movement. Who are these people? What would prompt them to do something so out of the ordinary, so countercultural? Do their children suffer academically or socially from the experience? Let's take a closer look at some of these questions.

Describing the typical home schooler is a particularly challenging task. With the advent of organized home school associations and their convenient membership rolls, home school researchers have found a readily accessible population from which to gather data. The vast majority of these associations are Christian based, so it is no surprise the data suggests that approximately 94 percent of American home schoolers are Protestant Christian. The data also suggests about 94 percent of American home schoolers are white.[4]

Determining just how representative those numbers are is problematic at best. How likely is it that a Jew, Muslim, or secular humanist would become an active member of a clearly Christian home school association? Additionally, is there a portion of the home schooling population (Christian or otherwise) that simply does not join any local organization? Could it be that the Christian population of home schoolers is simply the most organized?

Even within the population of those belonging to a home school association, you'll find a wide range of attitude and philosophy about educating children at home. Some people home school for brief periods; others are committed to home school for particular grades; still others are determined to home school all the way through high school. Some change their minds along the way. Some households may have older children in traditional school environments, while younger children are being home schooled. All of these possible variations prompted home school researcher Patricia Lines to state, "One of the most challenging aspects of home-school research relates to the difficulty in identifying the universe of home schoolers."[5]

Consider the case of Mrs. Cynthia Sulaiman. In some ways she fits a fairly common profile of a home educator, while in other ways she is probably somewhat unique. Cynthia lives in Massachusetts with her husband and four children. In 1994 she began home schooling and being the energetic person she is, that same year she founded MHSNR, a national organization to help link other like-minded home schoolers for the purpose of sharing resources and encouragement.[6] Mrs. Sulaiman states she was driven to her decision to home school by a concern for the quality of education available through the public schools as well as personal concerns about the spiritual development of her children.

Like many of her home schooling peers, Cynthia shops for the curriculum material that seems to best meet the needs of her children, sometimes using Christian materials like those produced by Abeka Publishing and at other times using nonsectarian textbooks. She has learned to pick and choose carefully, modifying materials to suit her own needs. She often gathers with others at the monthly home school association, which meets in the homes of other home schoolers or the city library. While most mothers do not launch national organizations, this is not the only thing that is unique about Mrs. Sulaiman.

As a Muslim she probably represents a segment of the home school population that researchers have not explored. The organization she founded, Muslim Home School Network and Resource (MHSNR), has a membership of three hundred and produces a journal directed to the unique concerns of the Muslim home school population. According to Mrs. Sulaiman, she continues to hear from Muslims who just found out about a home schooling organization within their faith community.

Researcher Maralee Mayberry attempted to access a New Age population of home schoolers in Oregon and was able to locate eight families willing to participate in her project.[7] While the number examined in her research was relatively small, she reports, "There are many such families who, because they are suspicious of social research and tend to be either nomadic or residing in areas that are extremely isolated, often remain anonymous." A descriptive study of home schoolers in Washington state led researcher Valerie Witt to observe, "It is impracticable to routinely stereotype homeschoolers—they come from heterogeneous backgrounds, philosophies, and locations."[8]

Because the profile of a typical home schooler is probably something of a phantom idea, it should be no surprise to learn that home schoolers offer a variety of reasons for educating at home. The following list, given in no particular order, is compiled from a number of studies designed to determine why home schoolers choose this course of education.[9]

1. Academic difficulties in their present educational environment
2. Health problems
3. Child felt ostracized by peers
4. Conflicts over school curriculum (i.e., sex education, evolution)
5. Conviction over fulfilling religious responsibility as parent
6. Threat of secular humanism
7. Desire to build family unity and strength
8. Protection from drugs, alcohol, and premarital sex
9. Seeking lower teacher-student ratio
10. Seeking individualized teaching methodology
11. Concern over moral or philosophical conflict
12. Physical safety
13. Special needs of the child (i.e., learning disability or giftedness)
14. Conflict with teacher

Looking over the list you can see that some motives are of a philosophical nature, while others are quite pragmatic. Van Galen has offered two useful categories of home schoolers—Ideologues and Pedagogues.[10] Ideologues are driven by philosophical or religious convictions, often having to do with values and beliefs they believe are not being taught at all in public schools or are being taught in a way that is inconsistent with their views. Pedagogues are less concerned about what is taught, but are critical of traditional classroom environments that they believe result in ineffective instruction.

In truth, most home educators offer multiple reasons for their choice. Thus, it is often a combination of concerns, held with varying degrees of conviction, that finally propels a parent toward a decision to educate their child at home. It is also worth noting the observation of researcher Mary Hood who observes, "Educational beliefs and assumptions do not necessarily coincide with the religious affiliations or beliefs held by the participants."[11] Thus, even within a local gathering of home schoolers in a decidedly Christian environment, a wide range of pedagogical and theological concerns can be represented.

Not only are multiple reasons often a part of the decision to home school, apparently those reasons are subject to change. In a study designed to ascertain reasons why parents choose to educate at home, Steven Gray discovered, "The reasons parents gave for beginning to home school were not always the same reasons that kept them home schooling."[12]

The picture of a typical home schooler that emerges is really a cut-and-paste collage of considerable diversity. Even among more homogenous subgroups of the home schooling population, such as conservative Christians or Muslims, a wide range of convictions are behind the decision to move away from the traditional classroom environment. At the same time, these convictions may be quite fluid, changing dramatically or simply sliding along a continuum of greater or lesser emphasis. Whatever the reasons, with the number of home schoolers approaching the two million mark, it's appropriate to ask how these children are doing, both academically and socially.

Imagine the consternation and skepticism among certified teachers when they are asked to believe that virtually any mom can teach her own children just as effectively as the professional teacher. Professional teachers take a series of university classes, each one including projects and exams and papers, and then endure student teaching just to graduate and get certified. Add to that years of experience that have sharpened their teaching skills. With so much criticism being leveled at America's public schools, the suggestion that untrained mothers are just as capable of teaching their children as their public school counterparts seems like an indictment of the whole public school enterprise. It's little wonder that home schooling has often met with resistance among the existing educational community.

It's also not surprising that researchers have done a lot of work to try to determine how home schooled children fare academically in comparison to their public schooled peers. The primary method researchers have used is to look at standardized tests. For example, tests like the Iowa Test of Basic Skills (ITBS) and the Stanford Achievement Test (SAT) are commonly given to many of the nation's public school children. By administering those same tests to home schooled children, scores could be compared with relative ease.

Researcher J. F. Rakestraw chose the Stanford Achievement Test to be the comparative instrument in a study involving eighty-four Alabama home schooled children.[13] The SAT scores from these children in grades one through six were compared to the scores of all Alabama public school children as well as to the national scores. Results indicated that home schooled children were at or above their grade level in nearly all subject

111

areas. In a separate study, also using the Stanford Achievement Test, the scores of 2,911 home schooled children were examined over a four-year period.[14] All of the children reached or exceeded the sixty-fifth percentile in all areas tested. The national average among public-schooled children was the fiftieth percentile. A smaller study in Pennsylvania yielded similar results.[15]

Researcher E. A. Frost opted for the Iowa Test of Basic Skills, administering it to home schooled children in a five-county region of northern Illinois.[16] Not only did the home schooled children all test higher than their current grade placement, they outscored their public school peers in the areas of vocabulary, reading, language skills, and work study skills.

In one of the most extensive studies to date, the ITBS was administered to over twenty thousand home schooled students, representing all grades and all fifty states.[17] The results are consistent with virtually every other study that has compared the academic success of home schooled children with their public school counterparts. This study reported that on average home school students in the first four grades perform one grade level above their public and private school peers. Further, by the time the home schoolers reach grade eight, on average they are four years ahead of public school students.

Over the last several decades a wealth of research on the academic progress of home schoolers has been compiled, producing a compelling picture of widespread success. The consistently high scores from home schoolers have prompted the president of the Home School Legal Defense Association, Michael Farris, to state summarily, "On average, home schoolers out-perform their public school peers by 30 to 37 percentile points across all subjects."[18] Apparently mothers are quite capable of effectively educating their children without the benefit of formal training. Indeed, researchers who examined the background of home schooling parents determined academic success was virtually unrelated to the lack of teacher certification or even the presence or absence of a college degree.[19]

Even though standardized test scores are readily available and represent a kind of stable, numerical value that is easily compared, they don't tell the whole academic story. Even among public school educators, there is ongoing dismay over the abuses of standardized test scores. The problem is that standardized tests only represent one piece of a complex pie. Areas such as creativity, critical thinking, physical abilities, work habits, and organizational skills are important targets of every educator but are much more difficult to evaluate through standardized testing. Because these pieces of the educational pie are more difficult to evaluate, less research is available that would compare public schooled and home schooled children in these important areas. While probably too scant to draw definitive conclusions, the following is a brief summary of research that does address these various categories.

Regarding critical-thinking skills, an interesting study was conducted in which 789 first-year college students were tested for their critical-thinking skills.[20] Public school students, Christian school students, and home school students were all compared with one another in this important area. No significant differences were found among any of the three groups. Whether the tested ability was to analyze, evaluate, infer, or use deductive/inductive reasoning, all three groups achieved essentially the same scores.

Child psychologist Richard Medlin explored the creative abilities of home schooled children.[21] Understanding that the fiftieth percentile represents the average score of students in public schools, he tested home

113

schoolers in the areas of math concepts, verbal creativity, and figural creativity. Results placed home schoolers well above the fiftieth percentile.

The development of physical fitness and motor skills has been the subject of a few researchers, and the results have been somewhat mixed. A Michigan study found home schooled students to perform "at a significantly lower level than the conventional school group in fundamental motor skill ability."[22] In another study, home schoolers were found to fall within the same range of body fat as their public school peers and to have comparable physical fitness and activity characteristics.[23]

These and other studies suggest there is more to a fully educated person than the simple memorization of facts and the ability to respond to those facts on a multiple choice test. Nevertheless, while there is still a lot of room for researchers to explore a more holistic picture of home schooling and what it means to be academically successful, home educating parents have reason to be encouraged. In light of the consistent evidence that home educated children seem to outperform their public school peers, at least on standardized tests, the voices of resistance to home schooling have sometimes redirected their concerns to something other than academic success.

Kindergarten and first-grade public school teachers may have one of the most difficult jobs in the world! Not only does their foundational instruction have enormous consequences for the years of education that lie ahead, they must accomplish this task with wiggly five-year-olds. It is hard to know what is most important at that age, learning the rudiments of reading or learning to pay attention and follow directions. You can hardly have one without the other. Thus, these early-childhood teachers work very diligently to establish the rules, norms, and expectations for behavior that make school possible. Learning to wait patiently, to take turns, to share, to recognize when it is okay to make noise and when it is time to be quiet, to keep your hands to yourself, to focus on the task at hand while others are busy around you, to respect the dignity and property of others, to accept authority and the consequences of inappropriate behavior—these are just a sampling of the essential lessons taught in those early years and reinforced throughout the public school experience.

In other words, along with the curriculum of reading and writing and mathematics, students also learn the social conventions necessary to get along with people. This issue of socialization concerns many critics of home schooling. How can a child possibly be expected to get along in life—the people side of life—if he or she has been isolated from the school environment that has shown the rest of us how it's done?

The socialization of children is a concept difficult to define, which makes research in this area a problem. We can hardly agree on what we mean by the term. For example, are we speaking of respect for others? If so, what does that look like? Does that mean saying "Yes, ma'am," and "Yes, sir?" Does that mean holding a door for someone? Taking turns? Sharing? How do you design a research study that measures manners among public schooled or home schooled children? Perhaps socialization is simply the absence of pushing, shoving, or doing physical harm to others that get in your way. Does it mean poise and confidence around people? If so, how do you measure poise or confidence? What about children who are quiet, reserved, and introverts by nature? How do we factor personality into our definition of socialization?

For others, socialization may be more about developing the characteristics of good citizenship. Some would argue the public school experience is the common ground we all share. We all learn to say the pledge of allegiance, to submit to authority, to follow the rules, and to learn the basic norms and values of American life that permeate the larger culture. As was pointed out in an earlier chapter, this kind of socialization was thought to be very important during the early formation of America's public school system. As throngs of non-English-speaking immigrants made their way to our shores, the public school system was seen as a primary mechanism for socializing these people into the norms and values inherent in the living definition of what it means to be an American. While somewhat less dramatic, the need was (and continues to be for those who define socialization in these terms) no less important for native-born children.

Of course the good-citizen approach to defining socialization has its own problems. Researchers are burdened with trying to define, with some meaningful precision, what we mean by "good citizenship." How do you evaluate patriotism? How much is enough patriotism? How do you evaluate how fervently a person embraces a particular cultural value? How do you measure any of these things so that researchers could compare a home schooled child with a public or private schooled child? Nevertheless, as problematic as defining socialization may be, a few researchers have made noble attempts to examine the matter. An overview of available research reveals the following.

A study done in 1986 represents one of the earliest attempts to examine the socialization of home schoolers.[24] The researcher viewed self-concept as a reasonable way to measure socialization because self-concept seemed to be closely tied to an individual's values, social competence, and self-evaluation. Home schooling parents from around the country were mailed the Piers-Harris Self-Concept Scale, which they administered to their children and returned by mail. Two hundred twenty-four home schooled children in grades four through twelve responded. Results show that these home educated children have a significantly higher self-concept overall, and they also scored higher on all six individual subscales than the norms of public school children.

In 1991, another researcher used the Piers-Harris Children's Self-Concept Scale to assess the self-concept of sixty-seven children being home schooled in suburban Los Angeles.[25] Results indicate that the home educated children scored significantly higher than the norms of conventionally schooled students.

Also in 1991, Paul Kitchen used the Self-Esteem Index, a standardized instrument that has been found to produce scores consistent with the Piers-Harris Children's Self-Concept Scale, to compare the self-esteem of home schooled children and conventionally schooled children in grades six through eight.[26] The home schooled children scored higher in every category except for peer popularity, where 9 percent more of the conventionally schooled children scored higher.

One of the most ambitious studies on home schoolers and socialization was done in 1992 by Larry Shyers. He compared the behaviors of seventy home schooled and seventy public schooled children. He matched all the children in terms of their age, gender, economic status, and residential setting. Shyers also used the Piers-Harris Children's Self-Concept Scale and found that both groups of children scored above the national average with no significant differences between the two groups.

More intriguing conclusions came from a second portion of the study. Shyers videotaped subjects as they interacted with one another in play activities prescribed by the researcher. Six home school children and six public school children at a time were placed in a room with instructions that allowed for children to either participate in the activities or to choose not to participate. Pairs of trained observers viewed the videotaped activities and recorded behaviors, not knowing which children were being educated at home and which were attending public schools. Results indicate that among the group of children examined, those "who have been educated entirely in traditional schools have problem behaviors that are above normal ranges for national populations," while those children who had been exclusively home schooled "had significantly fewer problem behaviors than children of the same age from traditional schools."[27]

This last finding presents us with an interesting question. Even if we could agree on what constitutes socialization, what is the best way to achieve that socialization? Is it wise to assume that public schools offer the best context for reaching our socialization goals? For home school advocates who are often asked the question, "What about the socialization of your children?" the response is often a simple, "Exactly!"

Home schooling parents, dismayed by what they believe to be an unacceptably negative social environment in the traditional classroom, would ask the same question asked by researcher Witt: "Are social skills best taught by caring nurturing adults, or immature peers who often lack the essential rudiments of getting along in an adult society?"[28]

In further defense of a home schooled version of socialization, researcher Tillman states, "Home schooling parents have a unique view of self-esteem and socialization. Rooted in the family and often in their faith, these parents seek to provide safe, secure, positive environments for their children to grow and learn. Children are encouraged to apply learned skills in the larger world as preparation for adulthood. This is their socialization."[29]

118

Nevertheless, while one might concede that the traditional classroom has its problems, how can a home schooled child learn any of the essential social skills when they are so isolated from interactions with other human beings? At least that much of the socialization question seems to have viable answers.

If interaction with other children is the key ingredient to socialization, home schoolers have found ways other than those of the traditional classroom to provide these experiences. One way this is done is through activities organized by local home school associations. These organizations are known to produce their own spelling and geography bees, science fair competitions, field trips, and physical education opportunities. Home school associations may also organize periodic classes in areas of parental expertise such as foreign language study, advanced science or math, or some practical skill. Another primary means of exposure to other children and adults is through extracurricular activities.

Researcher Smedley examined the extracurricular activities of thirty-three home schooled children and compared them to public schooled peers of the same religious and socioeconomic background.[30] It was found that public schooled children spent an average of 3.3 hours per week in extracurricular activities, while the average home schooler spent 4.2 hours per week in such activities. In a study of 259 home schooling families from the states of Delaware, Pennsylvania, and Maryland, researchers found the range of extracurricular activities was quite extensive.[31] Some of those activities, from this and similar studies, included:

Home school band
Civil air patrol cadets
Church musicals

Playing with friends and neighbors
Hospitality to foreign students and extended family
Overseas trips
Playgroups
Babysitting co-ops
Helping grandparents
Little League participation
Nursing home visits
Scouts
Community service
4-H Clubs

Not only do home schoolers appear to be quite busy socially, the activity seems to transcend age and gender barriers—a factor thought to be a real plus in the proper development of a child's social skills. Child psychologist Dr. Richard Medlin concluded from his own research that "home-schooled children regularly associated with adults outside their own family; the elderly; people from a different socio-economic, religious, or ethnic background than their own; and children attending conventional schools."[32] From the evidence available, it would appear home educated children are faring quite well in the area of socialization.

These children are not nearly as isolated from others, including their peers, as people may have assumed, and the quality of their social experiences is arguably more effective in developing the desired values and socialization skills. Indeed, many home schooling parents would argue that they are able to be far more thoughtful and deliberate in orchestrating healthy and positive socialization experiences for their child than they could if their child was attending a conventional school.

From the results of the research mentioned above, it would seem that home schooling is the way to go. Gone are the issues of large classrooms or even small classrooms for that matter. Concerns about bullies, drugs, negative peer pressure, inappropriate sex education, poor academic programs, and negative socialization issues seem to be eliminated by educating at home. And it would appear that the average mom is quite capable of producing excellent results. With so much to commend home schooling, you are left to wonder if there is a catch in all this. Is it all good news when it comes to home schooling?

Theodore Wade wrote and edited a book on home schooling back in 1984, when there was not a lot to be found for anyone considering teaching their children at home.[33] Wade titles one of his chapters "Not for Some Parents." To follow in boldface type are my own paraphrases of three of Wade's cautionary questions, with my own comments following each.

1. **Is there a personality conflict between you and your child?** Some well-meaning parents simply do not possess good parenting skills. To be fair, it is not unheard of for good parents to struggle with a difficult child. Sometimes the answer is not as simple as getting some extra counseling in the area of parenting skills. Whatever the explanation, if your day is marked by tension and conflict with your child, it may not be in the best interests of either of you to home school. This should not be used as an easy excuse to avoid the challenges of home schooling, but if necessary you should have the courage to choose another path.

2. **Are you very disorganized?** Home schooling calls for a good bit of planning and organization within the context of the many distractions found in a

typical home. Thoughtfully, Wade asks, "Do you tend to plan your time and follow through on your plan? Do you see the tasks you want to do as having various degrees of importance? . . . Are you the master of the TV and the telephone, or do they dictate what else you accomplish and when?"

While we all have various strengths and weaknesses in these areas, if organization is a genuine issue for you, home schooling may present an overwhelming challenge that results in a disservice to your child. It would be wise to talk with several other home schooling parents about the realities of educating your child at home to help you determine if this is the kind of activity to which you are suited.

3. **Are you fully committed to the task?** Home schooling can be labor-intensive and sometimes it can be discouraging. Wade states, "Unlike a hobby that can be put aside when it ceases to be fun, your school program requires steady rain-or-shine commitment." This is not to say there is no room for flexibility or days off, but this counsel is important. Educating your child at home is a big responsibility and should not be taken lightly.

More recently, researcher Steve Gray surveyed 144 home schoolers in California. He reported that "the main inconvenience cited by home schooling parents was time. The main hardship was financial."[34] Child psychologist Dr. Richard Medlin, himself a home schooler, conducted a survey of home schooling parents to determine the biggest challenges being faced.[35] His findings resonate with those of Gray. The top four home school difficulties given were:

1. Having enough time with my spouse and enough time alone

2. Avoiding interruptions during school time
3. Having enough time for other responsibilities and activities
4. Physical exhaustion

Over a third of those surveyed by Medlin indicated they did not know how long they would continue to home school. Researcher Mark Resetar reported similar findings after surveying sixty-six home schooling families. He reported 23.7 percent of surveyed parents indicated teaching at home is draining and time consuming.[36] It is important to understand that even though these parents acknowledge the exhausting demands home schooling can present, they are not necessarily sorry they chose this course of action. Nevertheless, a parent would be ill-advised to choose the home schooling option without having a realistic picture of what is involved.

Working with school officials may test your commitment to home schooling. Some people live in communities that are very hospitable to home schoolers. However, for some, the experience is quite the opposite. In a nationwide survey of school administrators, participants were asked to rank alternatives to public schools.[37] These school administrators indicated that they thought almost anything was better than home schooling. Despite the research to the contrary, over half said they believed home schooled students did not meet the academic standards set by their states.

In a survey of home schoolers in Washington state, 52.7 percent of those who filed letters of intent to home school with their local school districts found personnel to be indifferent, disapproving, and in some isolated instances hostile.[38] For today's home schooler, resources and support are available to help in overcoming bureaucracy or resistance, but parents should know that it may not always be easy or pleasant. Again, this is not necessarily a reason to avoid home schooling but is offered to help parents make an intelligent decision.

Finally, parents should consider an intangible but important component to home schooling. Because education is inescapably a human enterprise, it can be something of a messy business. This is true for the traditional classroom setting, but it is also true for home schooling. Some public or private school teachers seem to be well suited to a first-grade classroom but would be ineffective with middle school children. Some adults seem to make great Little League coaches, while others are wired to work with teens in a church youth group. In similar fashion, some parents are probably better wired by temperament and disposition to be effective home schoolers of their own children at certain ages, but not at other times.

Parents and children have different thresholds of patience, noise, adherence to routine, time on task, and a host of other issues. Home schooling is not a one-size-fits-all enterprise. It is not at all uncommon for home schooling parents to evaluate their particular situation and decide to release their home schooled child back to a traditional classroom. This traditional classroom arrangement may last a year or two with home schooling resumed at an appropriate time.

The key ingredient in any schooling choice, including home schooling, is the active participation of the parent. Home schooling is not some unique teaching method that produces high test scores. Its virtues and successes may have more to do with the unique parent-child relationship that is fostered than anything else. Some have speculated that home schooled children fare as well as they do not because they are home schooled but because they have parents who are deeply involved in their lives. This may strike closest to the heart of the matter and serves as a challenge to any who would choose this alternative to the traditional classroom.

124

Dodging the Silver–Bullet Mentality

Making Sense of It All

While surfing through television channels recently, my attention was momentarily captured by an intense scene in which three people were apparently trapped in a room with a werewolf. In the midst of the chaotic scrambling there was a gun and a separate, single bullet being fought over. One of the people ended up with the gun, but the bullet had fallen down a heat grating.

Because I had seen none of the story preceding this particular scene, I was left to wonder how there was an empty gun with only one bullet available. It was then that I remembered the legend that the only way to stop a werewolf is with a special silver bullet. Any other bullets were useless against a werewolf. Sure enough, at the last possible moment, one of the characters loaded this lone silver bullet, fired a shot, and saved the day.

It occurs to me that in real life people often approach a complex issue like schooling with a silver-bullet mentality. Some people would have us believe that a particular type of schooling embodies all that is wrong in education today (the werewolf), and the singular, silver-bullet solution to this calamity is their schooling choice. Life certainly would be a lot simpler if things were this black and white, but unfortunately this does not seem to represent accurately the reality most of us are living.

I often ask my seminary students to describe their ideal learning environment. It is not uncommon for these Christians to create a scenario in which they have several uninterrupted hours to ask Jesus Christ anything on their mind. You might select someone else, but the idea of being allowed to ask your most pressing or personal questions without competing with anyone else's time or attention seems to be the consummate learning opportunity.

However, others have suggested that this special educational moment could actually be improved a bit if you were to invite two or three others to join you. Why would this improve the situation? Because these additional participants would ask questions that you had not thought of asking but should have asked. Additionally, they would bring life experiences, perspectives, attitudes, and various levels of maturity to the situation that would enrich the interchange in ways that are not likely to happen if you were by yourself.

Upon further reflection, my seminary students typically relinquish the idea of a lone encounter and concede the wise addition of one or two others. At this point I invite them to consider what they are likely to have sacrificed by adding these extra folks. For example, not every person asks a brilliant question every time. Sometimes questions are important to those who asked them but not to you. At other times you may have already resolved the issue behind their question, and it is of little concern to you any longer. With two or three of you eager to ask follow-up questions, someone will have to wait their turn. You may find the first answer quite satisfactory and see no need for the follow-up question.

Graciously waiting for others means you lose the time and opportunity to ask more personally pressing questions. Of course, one could argue that it's important to learn to wait your turn and to understand that you are not, despite the desperate longings of your heart, the center of the universe. Nevertheless, you see how difficult it is to create an ideal learning environment, even in the imaginary world of magic wands and unlimited possibilities.

Why would we think it is any easier to fashion an educational silver bullet here in the real world of conflicting passions and human inconsistencies? And yet there are those who think that if we do not opt for their form of educational choice, we are letting the werewolf roam freely in our home. The intensity of the passions and the oversimplifications that are often associated with these issues can have a paralyzing effect on any well-intentioned parent who is trying to sort out the merits of one choice over another.

As demonstrated by seminary students, whether you send your child to the public schools, opt for a private school environment, or educate at home, you are always giving up something to get something. The preceding chapters have been my attempt to help you understand and weigh the seriousness of what you're giving up and getting with a particular educational choice. Let me add a few closing thoughts about each of the three choices most commonly available to parents.

Public Schools

As reported in *U.S. News and World Report*, only about 6 percent of Americans graduated from high school in

1900. By the 1950s that number had risen to 59 percent and by the beginning of the new millennium, over 80 percent of America's youth were graduating.[1] Despite its many problems, the enormous effort to educate every single boy and girl in America has been a noble undertaking. While we must not gloss over very real concerns about the state of today's public schools, we ought also to remember that good things happen every day in these same schools.

Sixty-five percent of the 1999 entering class at Harvard University came from America's public schools.[2] The same was true at Stanford University.[3] At MIT the number was 71 percent.[4] Whatever else might be said, it would appear that the majority of America's best and brightest (as represented by the rigorous entrance requirements at these prestigious universities) still come out of our public schools.

Does this mean that all the concern and rhetoric about the sad state of America's public schools is just so much bombast? Does this mean the odds are better that your child will flourish in a public school than with one of the other educational choices? Does this mean that everyone getting into a prestigious university has the moral character to match their academic accomplishments? No, of course not. But then the same could be said of the private school population and the home schoolers as well.

I regularly teach classes at a local university that are full of students well on their way to becoming public school teachers. In a recent class, I was sharing the research that seems to support the strong achievement of home schoolers. In an attempt to stimulate their thinking, I was lobbying rather forcefully for the virtues of this educational choice.

After listening patiently, one student raised her hand and rather heatedly stated, "If I had one or two children, instead of thirty, I could produce the same results. That mom is getting those results not because she is a brilliant teacher but because she has a huge numerical advantage over me." I found her emotional and defensive reaction both interesting and predictable. It doesn't take much to polarize people on these issues. Her comment, however, provoked a very interesting discussion that forced us to look for the realities of life that lie behind the use of test scores to support a particular position.

Educational policy in America is largely driven by test scores. Government funds are often tied to student achievement, which is almost always determined by some sort of standardized test. In some locations schools are assigned a grade, such as A or B or F, depending on student test scores.

These ever-present test scores are sometimes published in local newspapers to the glory or shame of teachers and school administrators. The alleged quality of schools in an area, almost always determined by test scores, impact real estate values. On the basis of test scores money is variously poured into failing systems, or withheld in some punitive attempt to admonish school personnel to get their act together. Test scores rule the day!

The first line of defense among home schoolers is often to cite test scores that show their children to be doing just fine, thank you. (Many home schoolers recognize the limitations of test scores but understand that this is the way the battle is being fought.) With so much at stake, we should ask ourselves just how much we should base our own decision on test scores.

When you administer a standardized test to a large group of people, like America's children, some kids are going to do very well, some won't, while others will have less extreme measures of success or failure. No matter how any particular child scores, they all go into one big pot to produce a national average.

To understand this average we have to appreciate the fact that some very bright, highly motivated students are pulling the scores up, producing a number that does not really represent the accomplishments of those less bright or less motivated students. At the same time, the very low scores of our most troubled students are dumped into the same pot. The general theory is that the very high and very low scores tend to neutralize each other and thus the average that finally emerges represents the typical student from the public school population. This is quite an assumption to make about millions of people. It's like saying the average white person smokes 3.7 cigarettes a day, the average Christian prays twice a month, or the average woman spends two hours a week on quilting. Millions of folks don't smoke at all, many Christians pray with daily regularity, and some ladies have never quilted a stitch.

Averages from large populations should be understood to have a wide variety of exceptions. For example, some students fail miserably in the public schools, while others soar. The explanation for why one fails and the other flourishes is lost in a sea of paper-and-pencil test scores where the entire population is represented by a singular average. Even the traditional public school population is realizing the misuse of standardized testing. *Time* magazine reported that a group in Massachusetts marched on the governor's mansion in protest, inviting the governor to take the state's required standardized test. The same article indicates that protest-the-test groups have emerged in at least thirty-six states.[5] You must ask yourself how much that test score really tells you about how your child will fare in a given educational setting.

For some parents, academic achievement is not the biggest concern. Numerous unofficial or intangible components of school life move parents to opt for private or home schooling for their child. For example, there is the matter of peer pressure, and how a parent sees their child either flourishing or struggling in this area. For others the issue might be that worldviews or religious convictions are either underrepresented or plainly opposed.

Still others steer away from traditional public schooling because of deep concern over character development. Does it matter that your child can recite from memory every state capital or score in the ninety-eighth percentile on a standardized test if their moral character is being undermined by a stream of negative influences? Former Secretary of Education, William Bennett, states, "The decisions we make about education are really decisions about our children's character and the architecture of their souls."[6]

I asked Ruth Ann Wells, home schooling mother of six, to talk to me about her reasons for choosing this route for her family. You will hear more from her later, but when asked about her reasons for home schooling, she said, "Character building is a big emphasis. Self-control, kindness, honesty, dependability, neatness, etc. Things that can make or break you in adulthood. Academics alone will not make anyone a success. I have seen brilliant people with no self-discipline go absolutely nowhere. That's not what we want for our kids. We want them to love God, to love others, to love learning, to be able to say no to themselves, to do right."[7]

For Mrs. Wells and many others, the best way to see that these character issues are properly taught is to do it at home where you can exercise more personal direction and control over these matters. In the end you may not feel you have to home school in order to accomplish these goals for your children, but I hope you will consider the issue with the same dedication that has driven Ruth Ann Wells to her particular educational choice.

Before we turn our attention away from public schools and toward private/Christian schools, I'd like to point out two relatively new variations on the traditional public school model that are increasingly being discussed by parents and educators. Charter schools and magnet schools have been the choice of some parents who are not yet ready to make a complete departure from the world of public schools.

Charter schools are public schools that have been granted permission to operate without many of the bureaucratic requirements normally associated with public schools. They typically petition the governing authorities for permission to operate and are granted approval based on the charter, or contract, which typically spells out the school's mission, the particular students it intends to serve, its program, and the methods for evaluating performance.

The understanding is that if the school meets the stated performance goals, the charter will be renewed. Otherwise the school will be closed. As stated by the U.S. Department of Education, "The basic concept of charter schools is that they exercise autonomy in return for this accountability."[8] Educators Good and Braden observe that "the belief that a market-driven organization will outperform a traditional bureaucratic model is fundamental to the movement."[9]

The existence of charter schools is a fairly recent phenomenon, and as such is experiencing its own set of growing pains. According to a Gallup Poll, over half of America's parents with children in the public schools had never even heard about charter schools.[10] Among those who had, nearly half did not favor the idea. Minnesota passed the first charter school law in 1991 with

California following suit the next year.[11] As of this writing, thirteen states still have no laws allowing for the existence of such schools.

Even among states that do have laws allowing for charter schools, eagerness to establish charter schools varies. Arizona leads the way with 433 charter schools as of September, 2001, although California boasts the largest charter school enrollment with almost 74,000 students.[12] Arizona, California, and Michigan enroll over half of the nation's charter school students.[13] At the same time, Indiana, New Hampshire, and Wyoming have charter school laws in place, but not a single charter school has been launched.[14] Arkansas's charter school law existed for four years before the first charter school came into existence.[15] Many other states operate but a handful.

Does the charter school alternative present a viable option for parents searching for the best educational experience for their child? That is a difficult question to answer and will depend a great deal on the specific choices available to you where you live. The charter school landscape is so varied that once again the burden falls heavily on you, the parent, to do your homework and stay involved all along the way. Consider the following information gleaned from current research:

1. The *Orlando (Fla.) Sentinel* newspaper did an analysis of the statewide standardized testing of its students and found that 80 percent of the students in the state's charter schools scored lower than their traditionally schooled counterparts in one of three areas tested. Additionally, more than a third of the charter school students scored lower in all three categories.[16]

2. Cathy Wooley-Brown, charter school coordinator for the Florida State Department of Education,

said many of the charter schools opened hoping to attract students with strong academic skills. Instead, they became the last resort for the parents of struggling students.[17]

3. "The data shows conclusively that charter schools have made an indelible mark on education. Findings continue to reinforce the facts: charter schools are working, parents are happy about them, traditional school districts have been propelled to make improvements and children are thriving in a charter school setting," observed Center for Education Reform president, Jeanne Allen.[18]

4. Most charters serve students persistently underserved by the current system including at-risk, minority, and low-income students.[19]

5. Though thirty-eight states now have laws allowing charter schools, in many the chartering authorities are the biggest enemies of the charter schools.[20]

6. Charters vary in scope and mission, but that's because the essence of charters is a rejection of the establishment's one-size-fits-all approach. At the Pioneer Youth Corps Military Academy in Eugene, Oregon, four out of five students fall below the poverty level, and nearly half have had a brush with the law. By contrast, the Arizona School for the Arts, one of the top four schools in the state, teaches gifted students.[21]

7. Charters often must find their own facilities and finance them without additional assistance. In fact, less than a fifth of charter schools indicate they received any capital budget funds at all.[22]

8. Students choose to attend and teachers choose to teach at charter schools. Nearly 70 percent of charter schools have a waiting list equal to their enrollment.[23]

I trust that the mixed message of the above eight snapshots from current research alerts you to the need to be diligent when considering the charter school option. It is probably fair to say that because of the relatively brief track record of charter schools in America, it is difficult to make any safe generalizations about the overall success or failure of the idea. This assessment is echoed by educator Jeanne Allen. "While better student achievement is the goal of all charter schools, their relative newness and variations from state to state in assessing schools have made it difficult to draw any universal conclusions."[24]

If you are presented with a local charter school option that sounds appealing, I encourage you to visit the campus personally, talk to teachers and administrators, and gather as much firsthand information as possible. Once you opt for a charter school, stay diligently alert and involved.

Magnet schools have been around longer than charter schools, emerging back in the 1970s, initially as a means for addressing desegregation issues. The basic idea was to take an existing public school and alter its curriculum emphasis to make it attractive to those outside the immediate district. Thus a magnet school might decide to offer special classes in technology or theater arts, making the course of study so attractive that white students would be willing to drive to inner-city locations to enroll. This original purpose for magnet schools has evolved, prompting Dr. Donald Waldrip to observe, "Today magnet schools are still used to reduce racial isolation, but they are more and more considered superior options within the public sector for all students, even in districts of primarily one race."[25]

Today magnet schools are thought to be distinguished by at least three characteristics:[26]

1. There is a unified curriculum based on a special theme or method of instruction.
2. Enrollment is open to students beyond the geographic attendance zone.
3. Students and parents choose the school.

Many magnet schools require some form of entrance test for enrollment. At a school that emphasizes music or theater, there may be a performance tryout. For others it may be a paper-and-pencil test. Some have suggested that because not everyone gets into a magnet school, the school atmosphere is much more positive than the typical public school setting. As educator Morton Inger points out, "Because more students apply than get accepted, students who are admitted, and teachers who teach in a magnet, feel special about themselves and their school."[27] This is because, in part, "with very rare exceptions, students with failing grades, or records of bad behavior or truancy, do not get selected in magnets."[28]

How effective are magnet schools? Because magnet schools can vary so dramatically in their emphasis, it is difficult to compare one to another. Limiting yourself to the basic subjects of reading and math, at least one study found that "80 percent of the magnet schools had average reading and math achievement scores above their district average."[29] A more useful conclusion is probably rendered by researcher R. A. Dentler, who states, "Most magnets, like most nonmagnets, vary tremendously in their ability to deliver high educational quality."[30] Like charter schools, the potential benefit of a local magnet school must be evaluated carefully, recognizing once again that parental diligence is essential to any successful school experience.

Whether you find yourself leaning toward the traditional public school setting or some current variation available where you live, be encouraged. You are not alone. It has been estimated that 90 percent of Christian families in this country continue to send their children to public schools.[31] Countless thousands of single mothers probably have little choice in the matter. Others have extenuating circumstances in their lives that make private schooling or home schooling seem like an unavailable choice. Some parents simply have never thought about it much one way or the other. However, it is also safe to say that some very committed parents, like the Old Testament professor in the office next to mine, prayerfully gathered all the information at their disposal and chose public schools.

Private/Christian Schools

The financial side of private education has led some to see this alternative to the public schools as an option reserved only for the economically advantaged. Of course, only you can determine the nature and extent of the financial sacrifice you may have to make to exercise this option. However, it is not at all uncommon for many parents to have to cut corners, work overtime, and sacrifice some of their lifestyle choices in order to cover tuition costs. Logic suggests this sort of sacrificial commitment would be indicative of the heightened parental involvement that is bound to translate into a better educated child in every sense of the word. Each time that tuition check is put in the mail, the financial consequences can serve as a reminder to the family that they are on a bit of an educational mission. Ironically, there is the possibility that just the opposite may occur. Let me explain.

As a former public school teacher, I can tell you that it is a fairly universal lament among public school educators that parents seem to drop their kids off at school

137

with the idea that they have fulfilled their role in the educational effort. Would it surprise you to learn that a similar lament is heard from some private/Christian school teachers?

I don't mean to say private schools are no different than public schools when it comes to parental involvement. Overall, tuition-paying parents do tend to be more tuned in to their children's progress. Additionally, some private schools make certain parent involvements a condition of continued enrollment. Nevertheless, something about the financial sacrifice and all the accompanying mental and emotional effort that goes into the decision tempts some parents to drop their children off at school and drive off thinking they've fulfilled their role in their child's education. The temptation is to think you've done your part by sacrificially getting your child to the schoolhouse door, and now it is up to the private school to do their part. Between that temptation and a life full of activity, it is not difficult to imagine how a parent can drift away from full engagement in their child's education.

As was suggested in the chapter on private/Christian schools, this alternative to the public schools does not automatically mean immunity from negative peer pressure, bad language, bullying, cheating, crude humor, sexual innuendo or harassment, religious or values conflict, poor teaching, fights in the hall, poor sportsmanship, inefficient use of time, too much or too little homework, janitors having a bad day, and countless other concerns that attend life in school. Private schools typically have the freedom from governmental micromanagement to attempt to create a school culture that addresses these concerns. They also have the freedom to invite patrons to take their business elsewhere if a particular parent insists on having it their way. Nevertheless, even with strenuous efforts from everyone to be singing off the same page, sustained or complete success is elusive. This is because education is inescapably about people, and we're all different.

America's public schools represent the concept of the grand melting pot as well as any American institution. In Peoria, Illinois, there are a reported forty-eight different languages represented among its public school student body.[32] Denver, Colorado, reports eighty different languages in its schools,[33] and Orange County, Florida, reports 143.[34] It is easy to imagine the enormous diversity among cultures, worldviews, attitudes, and values found in this complex population.

When a parent moves their child to a private school, perhaps even a Christian school, it is reasonable to expect that the range of diversity will be reduced. In some Christian schools, for example, enrollment may be contingent on at least one of the parents being a professing Christian. Some Christian schools narrow the field even further, insisting that the parent be a member in good standing of the church that sponsors the school. Certain schools may require that all teachers be a member of the sponsoring church. In these cases, it is not unheard of for parents and children and teachers to see each other regularly in church and at various church functions, as well as during the school week. For many, this is the kind of unique educational environment they are seeking to buy with their tuition money.

It seems natural enough to make any number of assumptions about the values, beliefs, attitudes, and behaviors common to this particular group of people. However, even in a population as seemingly homogenous as the one described, there can be great diversity. For example, not every Christian (or Muslim or Jew) holds the same convictions about how Christmas ought to be celebrated, whether evolution ought to be avoided or confronted, what is acceptable television viewing, how to respond to a bully, what are appropriate extracurricular activities, control of peer pressure, classroom decorum, what constitutes too much homework, proper forms of rewards and punishments, and all the rest.

Because we Christians still wrestle with sin, we can be argumentative, prideful, and inconsistent. We get tired and cranky and critical. We bring our own emotional struggles to work, and we have bad days. We can be inconsistent in our own efforts to live out our convictions. This is true for parents, students, teachers, administrators, and all the support staff. Hopefully, these same Christians will be quick to acknowledge their mistakes, to extend forgiveness, and to get back on track. We can hope that in the final analysis this may be a wonderfully rich component of their education as students learn to give expression to their faith in a world of failure and conflict.

At the same time, where these matters are not dealt with or handled poorly, what students learn may have rather negative implications for their spiritual growth. Not all private schools hit the mark and that includes Christian schools as well. In those cases where Christian school is not done well, some would suggest the student would have been better off in the public schools where they aren't constantly being exposed to woefully bad examples of the Christian life.

How will you as a parent know if the Christian school you have selected is living up to your expectations? You won't know by its general reputation in the community, by its colorful brochure, by your friend's experience with her first-grader, or even by the seemingly benign comments from your own child at the end of a school day. The only way you can hope to provide the kind of education for your child that has motivated you to send your child to a private school in the first place is to exercise the same vigilant care and active involvement you would have needed to provide in the public school setting. This is as true for a Christian school as it is for a Hebrew Day School, a Muslim school, or a nonsectarian school. There is no silver bullet that will deliver you from the privileged burden of parental responsibility.

Home Schooling

Home schoolers have fought and scrambled for the last several decades for the right to educate their children at home. Opposition has come from both the professional educator and the average person on the street. Home schooling has often been characterized as a strange and misguided practice on the part of an irresponsible minority on the fringes of American culture.

While opposition has quieted in certain quarters, and despite the fact that the number of home schoolers is approaching the two million mark, home schoolers are still a distinct minority, and they continue to attract naysayers. If you have been talking to family and friends about these issues, you have probably run into a well-meaning colleague that has some caution or concern or negative opinion to share about that home schooling thing. For this reason, it seemed important for me to share with you the positive aspects of home schooling, as I did in the preceding chapter. It would be unfortunate if you dismissed home schooling as a very real educational option for your child because of misinformation or ignorance. However, it would be a disservice to you to leave you thinking home schooling is that elusive silver bullet. It is not.

Educating your child at home seems to eliminate so many of the problems we have been discussing in preceding chapters. As I pointed out earlier, class size is a non-issue. Issues of violence and drugs and sexual harassment and time spent waiting for classmates all seem to be gone from the home school scenario. Not only that, but who knows a child better than a well-intentioned parent? There is certainly the potential to tailor a lesson to meet the child's temperament or mood at the moment. There are opportunities for a parent's touch, a timely hug, and a special word of encouragement at just the perfect moment. As the parent, you are more in touch with your child to recognize those needs and because you don't have a whole class to contend with, you can make sure that the need of the moment is addressed.

A parent can cut a lesson short if she sees fit or extend a lesson for hours if a teachable moment emerges. Curriculum can be embraced or thrown away at will. These are all options that the classroom teacher must live without. Flexibility is everywhere for the home schooler. And of course there are those impressive test scores we looked at in a preceding chapter. How can you go wrong with home schooling? It's easier than you might think.

When listing the alleged benefits of home schooling, we are assuming a parent who actually does these things—a parent who is so tuned in to his or her child at all times that those magical moments pour forth in an endless stream of affirmation and just-right teachable moments. Is this what it is really like for the average home schooler? It's hard to say with certainty because there is no test to measure such things. But common sense suggests this picture-perfect education is not the reality. Are some days just not very productive? Are some days more accurately characterized by fussing and resistance to school work and half-hearted effort? Most home schoolers I know would readily concede.

I asked a few of my home schooling friends to consider what they might say to a parent considering this educational option. More particularly, I asked them to think about the negatives, the warnings, and the pitfalls that they would want a beginning home schooling parent to know about. I did not invite them to try to talk you out of it. Indeed, the following comments come from staunchly committed home schoolers. I did, however, invite them to alert you to some realities you would not necessarily be able to read about in the latest research. Consider the comments of Donna Joy Boxerman, pastor's wife and home schooling mother of four. Mrs. Boxerman has a master's degree in math and has taught both public and private school.

Some days the child doesn't understand what the parent is trying to explain. While they won't complain too boisterously to teachers, they'll indulge in major whining when it's just Mom and sometimes they won't even try to understand.

Sometimes the children say they're done, and Mom decides to check it later because if they don't leave now, they will be late for piano or soccer or whatever the activity of the day might be. Later, when Mom checks over the work, it turns out that someone was calling unfinished work "done" or was writing answers like "I don't know."

Some children are easily distracted. When there is only one child, you can stay on them. But in any other situation (public, private, or home), as soon as your back is turned (answering the phone, helping another child, or changing a baby's diaper), they're doodling all over their paper or book, staring into space.

When I taught public and private school and returned papers for do-overs because it was sloppy or done wrong or they didn't show work, the kids would fix them (even though they were pretty upset about it). At home they let me know how upset about it they are. If you're juggling a lot of things, sometimes it's easier to let it slide.

Mrs. Boxerman participates in a local home school organization that gets together regularly. Sometimes the parents teach each other's children in areas of expertise. Donna Joy typically teaches math and has made a few observations from this particular activity.

> I've observed that every parent has his strengths and weaknesses but in many cases, parents just give up on their weaknesses or things they don't want to teach and either don't teach them or hire anyone else to. I have come across hideously inadequate math skills, sloppy spelling, weak basic math facts, poor punctuation, sloppy handwriting, and poor vocabulary.
>
> I ran into kids who didn't understand the concept of "homework." Or high schoolers who couldn't follow directions. An American Government class was told to write a paper about someone for a minimum of two full pages. Only one child wrote at least two full pages. All the rest did a half to a whole page. One chemistry teacher had to require parents to initial each day's assignment to make sure it got done.
>
> I love home schooling, but it upsets me how slack some of us are.[35]

What are we to make of these comments? Should we take a deep breath and smugly say, "Ah-ha! I thought it was too good to be true. I knew that home schooling stuff was bogus." I certainly hope not. Perhaps I should also point out that Donna Joy loves home schooling and continues to think it is the best choice for her family.

What you should realize, however, is that there is no silver bullet to this question of how to educate your child and that includes the home schooling option. Because even the brightest and best-intentioned among us are human beings, we will falter and fail and have bad days. Consider the comments of Ruth Ann Wells, home schooling mother of six.

I find myself feeling like a failure a lot because I didn't accomplish what I had hoped to, having multiple interruptions and unexpected demands (sick kids, running a tool to my husband on the job, out-of-town company, doctor visits, etc.). I don't think I have been able to do much planning (which used to be a strength of mine) for the schooling needs of the kids and often feel very fly-by-night.

I get frustrated when I can't focus on a child without losing control of the others. So much to juggle and keep track of. I have trouble keeping track of papers, grading to see if they are really getting it. I can't find stuff, assignment sheets get lost. Etc. Not to mention regular household survival—laundry, dishes, meals, shopping, clean-up, bills, etc. I don't feel I have time enough to get my head together to plot a better strategy for getting all these things done.[36]

Again, these comments should not lead you to conclude that home schooling is a poor choice. I could share similar comments from scores of home schoolers I know, and you could be left with a very discouraging picture of this educational option. However, what would be true of every one of these home schooling parents is their undeniable commitment to the choice they have made. Trials and difficulties do not make public, private, or home schooling a poor choice. Trials and difficulties simply tell us that there is no silver-bullet solution and that as a parent you are going to have to fight the good fight whatever your choice.

My challenge to you as a parent is to educate yourself as thoroughly as possible about the educational options available to you, and then to muster the courage to make your decision independent of those who would do your thinking for you. Part of your task is learning to resist the shallow thinking that sometimes accompanies the latest test score or sound bite. Choosing to swim against the tide may mean patiently listening to some shrill voices of criticism, but do it anyway. As one writer put it, "No other arena of politics excites as much passion and stirs as many furious ideological clashes as the education of our children."[37]

In the end, how does it help you to know that Billy Graham graduated from a public high school or that Einstein failed in a public school setting? A recently discovered website contains a list of Nobel-prize winners with accompanying quotes in which they say how much they hated school.[38] Entertaining perhaps, but helpful? How does it help you to know that the winner of the national spelling bee in 2000 was home schooled as were the first and second runners up?[39] Are we to believe that the winner would not have won if he had not been home schooled? Are we to believe, on the other hand, that being home schooled had nothing to do with his success? Wouldn't this whole issue be much simpler if it were just a matter of black and white, cause and effect?

I suspect that as we move across the educational landscape we will find students flourishing and floundering in every setting. I firmly believe that the wild card in all cases is the involvement of the parent. Show me a child that is excelling, that is maturing into a well-informed and healthy person, and I will commend the parents who are most likely pouring their lives into the child. I encourage you to do your homework diligently as you make the decision about the educational setting that is best for your family. I encourage you then to pour yourself into your child's life on a daily basis. It is a wonderful privilege and responsibility, and, simply put, it works.

Earlier I quoted Ruth Ann Wells, a home schooling parent. I would like to conclude with some comments she shared with me. She happens to be in home schooling, but I trust you can hear the word of exhortation and hope that applies to every parent, no matter what the educational choice is.

In my early years, I was more militant about home schooling—every God-fearing family should do it. Not so now. My husband and I see it as a calling; a calling that each family has to pray through for each of their children. And it could change several times. The point is that parents are responsible for their children's education. What has been good for one child may not be good for the next. I find that we are continually going back to the Lord about each child because the task otherwise would be overwhelming. I keep in mind that these children have been given to us by God to raise. They were His first. I trust that He will direct our paths.[40]

Notes

Introduction

1. Institute of Urban Life, Loyola University, Chicago, "Chicago's Private Elementary and Secondary Schools: Their Role in Neighborhood Revitalization" (Chicago: Loyola University, 1998), 1.

Chapter 2: Why the Fuss?

1. Rudolf Flesch, *Why Johnny Can't Read* (New York: Harper and Row, 1955), 28.

2. Flesch, *Why Johnny Still Can't Read: A New Look at the Scandal of Our Schools* (New York: Harper and Row, 1981), 28.

3. Daniel Pedersen, "Tragedy in a Small Place," *Newsweek*, 15 December 1997, 30.

4. Gordon Witkin et al., "Again," *U.S. News & World Report*, 1 June 1998, 16.

5. David Brauer and John McCormick, "The Boys behind the Ambush," *Newsweek*, 6 April 1998, 20.

6. Patricia King and Andrew Murr, "The Killing Season," *Newsweek*, 1 June 1998, 33.

7. Ibid.

8. Nancy Gibbs, "Special Report: The Littleton Massacre," *Time*, 3 May 1999, 25.

9. Mitch Lipka, "Lake Worth Boy, 13, Guns Down Teacher," *Orlando Sentinel*, 21 May 2000.

10. Irwin A. Hyman, Avivah Dahbany, Michael Blum, Erica Weiler, Valerie Brooks-Klein, and Fariann Pokalo, *School Discipline and School Violence* (Boston: Allyn and Bacon, 1997), 309.

11. Mary Jo Nolin, Elizabeth Davies, and Kathryn Chandler, "Student Victimization at School" (report of the Department of Education, Office of Educational Research and Improvement, October 1995), 1.

12. Craig R. Sautler, "Standing Up to Violence," *Phi Delta Kappan* 76 (January 1995), in Lyndon G. Furst, "When Children Assault Children: Legal and Moral Implications for School Administrators," *Education Law Reporter* 13 (21 September 1995): 13.

13. Lowell C. Rose and Alec M. Gallup, "The 30th Annual Phi Delta Kappa/Gallup Poll of the Public's Attitudes toward the Public Schools," *Phi Delta Kappan* 80 (September 1998): 51.

14. Gordon Bachus, "Violence Is No Stranger in Rural Schools," *The School Administrator* 51 (1994): 19.

15. Lyndon G. Furst, "When Children Assault Children: Legal and Moral Implications for School Administrators," *Education Law Reporter* 13 (21 September 1995): 13.

16. Rose and Gallup, "Public's Attitudes toward the Public Schools," 46.

17. Nolin, Davies, and Chandler, "Student Victimization at School," 2.

18. "The American Psychological Association, Violence and Youth: Psychology's Response," *Summary Report of the American Psychological Association Commission on Violence and Youth*, vol. 1 (1993): 42, in Mary Jo Nolin, Elizabeth Davies, and Kathryn Chandler, "Student Victimization at School" (report of the Department of Education, Office of Educational Research and Improvement, October 1995), 1.

19. Albert Shanker, "Classrooms Held Hostage," *American Educator* 19 (1995): 8.

20. Nan Stein, Nancy L. Marshall, and Linda R. Tropp, "Sexual Harassment in Our Schools: A Report on the Results of a Seventeen Magazine Survey" (report of the Center for Research on Women at Wellesley College and NOW Legal Defense and Education Fund, 1993), 24.

21. Myra and David Sadker, *Failing at Fairness: How America's Schools Cheat Girls* (New York: Charles Scribner's Sons, 1994).

22. Nan Stein, "Sexual Harassment in School: The Public Performance of Gendered Violence," *Harvard Educational Review* 65 (1995): 153.

23. Valerie E. Lee, Robert G. Croninger, and Eleanor Linn, "The Culture of Sexual Harassment in Secondary Schools," *American Educational Research Journal* 33 (summer 1996): 398.

24. Ibid., 405.

25. "In Our Own Backyard: Sexual Harassment in Connecticut's Public High Schools," *Permanent Commission (CT) on the Status of Women* (Hartford, Connecticut, 1995), in Nan Stein, "Sexual Harassment in School: The Public Performance of Gendered Violence," *Harvard Educational Review* 65 (summer 1995): 152.

26. Stein, Marshall, and Tropp, "Sexual Harrassment in Our Schools," 4.

27. Ilene R. Berson, Michael J. Berson, Linda Karges-Bone, and Jonathan K. Parker, "Screening Teacher Education Candidates for Sexual Predators," *The Educational Forum* 63 (winter 1999): 152.

28. Charol Shakeshaft and Audrey Cohan, "Sexual Abuse of Students by School Personnel," *Phi Delta Kappan* 76 (March 1995): 515.

29. Hyman et al., *School Discipline and School Violence*, 318.

30. Ibid.

Chapter 3: So Much Time, So Little Learning!

1. James F. Bauman, "Implications for Reading Instruction from the Research on Teacher and School Effectiveness," *Journal of Reading* 28 (1984): 109–115.

2. Robert W. Gaskins, "The Missing Ingredients: Time on Task, Direct Instruction, and Writing," *The Reading Teacher* 41 (1988): 751.

3. Lyndall H. Rich and Mary J. McNelis, "A Study of Academic Time-On-Task in the Elementary School," *Educational Research Quarterly* 12 (1987–1988): 40.

4. U.S. Department of Education, National Commission on Excellence in Education, *A Nation at Risk: The Imperative for Educational Reform: A Report to the Nation and the Secretary of Education* (Washington, D.C.: GPO, 1983).

5. Emeral A. Crosby, "The 'At-Risk' Decade," *Phi Delta Kappan* 74 (1993): 604.

Chapter 4: Beyond the Three R's

1. Robert Rosenthal and Lenore Jacobsen, *Pygmalion in the Classroom: Teacher Expectation and Pupils' Intellectual Development* (New York: Holt, Rinehart and Winston, Inc., 1968), 175.

2. Lee Jussim and Jacquelynne S. Eccles, "Teacher Expectations II: Construction and Reflection of Student Achievement," *Journal of Personality and Social Psychology* 63 (1992): 953.

3. Vicki Ritts, Miles L. Patterson, and Mark E. Tubbs, "Expectations, Impressions, and Judgments of Physically Attractive Students: A Review," *Review of Educational Research* 62 (1992): 415.

4. R. C. Chia, L. J. Allred, W. F. Grossnickle, and G. W. Lee, "Effects of Attractiveness and Gender on the Perception of Achievement-Related Variables," *The Journal of Social Psychology* 138 (1998): 475.

5. Stuart J. McKelvie, "Perception of Faces with and without Spectacles," *Perceptual and Motor Skills* 84 (1997): 497.

6. Roger L. Terry and Lesley A. Stockton, "Eyeglasses and Children's Schemata," *The Journal of Social Psychology* 133 (1993): 425.

7. Nancy Eisenberg, Karlsson Roth, Karyl A. Bryniarski, and Edward Murry, "Sex Differences in the Relationship of Height to Children's Actual and Attributed Social and Cognitive Competencies," *Sex Roles* 11 (1984): 719.

8. Kate Eames and Kate Loewenthal, "Effects of Handwriting and Examiner's Expertise on Assessment of Essays," *The Journal of Social Psychology* 130 (1990): 831.

9. Herbert Harari and John W. McDavid, "Name Stereotypes and Teachers' Expectations," *Journal of Educational Psychology* 65 (1973): 222–25.

10. Andrew N. Christopher, "The Psychology of Names: An Empirical Reexamination," *Journal of Applied Social Psychology* 28 (1998): 1174.

11. Albert Mehrabian and Marlena Piercy, "Positive or Negative Connotations of Unconventionally and Conventionally Spelled Names," *The Journal of Social Psychology* 133 (1992): 447.

12. Thomas V. Busse and Louisa Seraydarian, "First Names and Popularity in Grade School Children," *Psychology in the Schools* 16 (1979): 149.

13. Gary S. Garwood, Valerie Kaplan, Neal Wasserman, and Jefferson L. Sulzer, "Beauty Is Only 'Name' Deep: The Effect of First-Name on Ratings of Physical Attraction," *Journal of Applied Social Psychology* 10 (1980): 433.

14. Pauline E. Henderson, "Communication without Words," *Personnel Journal* 68 (1989): 22.

15. Elisha Babad, Frank Bernieri, and Robert Rosenthal, "Students as Judges of Teachers' Verbal and Nonverbal Behavior," *American Educational Research Journal* 28 (1991): 213.

16. William Kilpatrick, *Source Book in the Philosophy of Education* (New York: Macmillan Company, 1923), in Peter S. Hlebowitsh, "The Forgotten Hidden Curriculum," *Journal of Curriculum and Supervision* 9 (1994): 347.

17. Catherine Cornbleth, "Beyond Hidden Curriculum?" *Journal of Curriculum Studies* 16 (1984): 33.

18. John Taylor Gatto, *Dumbing Us Down* (Philadelphia: New Society Publishers, 1992), 15–16.

19. *Teacher of the Year*, prod. Focus on the Family, 1990, videocassette.

20. Peter Hlebowitsh, "The Forgotten Hidden Curriculum," *Journal of Curriculum and Supervision* 9 (1994): 349.

Chapter 5: The Parental Factor

1. Katherine Lynn Lauderdale and Carlos A. Bonilla, "Hello Parents, Where Are You? A Teachers' Call for Involvement" (Stockton, Calif.: ICA Publishing, Stockton, 1998), ERIC, ED 422124, 45–46.

2. Jill Waterman, "Understanding the Impact of Parent School Involvement on Children's Educational Outcomes," *The Journal of Educational Research* 91 (1998): 378.

3. "Parent Involvement: The Key to Student Success and Community Support," <http://www.sdcoe.k12.ca.us/notes/4/parent-involv.html> (November 2001).

4. Vickie Lynne Luchuck, "The Effects of Parent Involvement on Student Achievement" (master's thesis, Salem-Teikyo University, 1998), 14.

5. Christine Winquist Nord, "Father Involvement in Schools" (Washington, D.C.: U.S. Department of Education, June 1998), ERIC, ED 419632, 3.

6. Christine Winquist Nord, "Nonresident Fathers Can Make a Difference in Children's School Performance: Issue Brief" (Washington, D.C.: National Center for Education Statistics, June 1998), ERIC, ED 420447, 2.

7. Esther Ho Sui-Chu and Douglas J. Willms, "Effects of Parental Involvement on Eighth-Grade Achievement," *Sociology of Education* 69 (1996): 138.

8. Karen J. Wells, "Professional Development for Parents," *The American School Board Journal* 184 (1997): 39.

9. Susan Black, "Parent Support," *The American School Board Journal* 185 (1998): 50.

10. Howard Kirschenbaum, "Night and Day: Succeeding with Parents at School 43," *Principal* 78 (1999): 20.

Chapter 6: How Did We Get Here?

1. C. Bishop, "Home Schooling Parent Support Groups in Kansas: A Naturalistic Inquiry into Their Concerns and Functions" (Ph.D. diss., Kansas State University, 1991).

2. Kenneth O. Gangel and Warren S. Benson, *Christian Education: Its History and Philosophy* (Chicago: Moody Press, 1983), 233.

3. Lawrence A. Cremin, *The Transformation of the School: Progressivism in American Education* (New York: Vintage Books, Random House, 1964), in Andrew Gulliford, *America's Country Schools* (Colorado: University Press of Colorado, 1996), 40.

4. Andrew Gulliford, *America's Country Schools* (Colorado: University Press of Colorado, 1996), 40.

5. Vance E. Randall, "The State and Religious Schools in America: An Overview of a Rocky Relationship," *Journal of Research on Christian Education* 3 (1994): 181.

6. Lawrence A. Cremin, *American Education: The Metropolitan Experience 1876–1980* (Philadelphia: Harper and Row, 1988), 3.

7. Joseph Newman, *America's Teachers: An Introduction to Education* (New York: Longman, 1990), 137.

8. J. F. Rakestraw and D. A. Rakestraw, "Home Schooling: A Question of Quality, an Issue of Rights," *The Educational Forum* 55 (1990): 69.

9. Cremin, *American Education*, 305.

10. Ibid., 297.

11. Gulliford, *America's Country Schools*, 35.

12. Joseph W. Newman, "Comparing Private Schools and Public Schools in the 20th Century: History, Demography and the Debate Over Choice," *Educational Foundations* 9 (1995): 9.

13. *Meyer v. Nebraska*, 262 U.S. 390 (1923).

14. *Pierce v. Society of Sisters*, 268 U.S.510 (1925), in Christopher J. Klicka, *The Right to Home School* (Durham, N.C.: Carolina Academic Press, 1998), 34.

15. *People v. Levisen*, 404Ill. 574, 90 N.E.2d 213 (1950), in Christopher J. Klicka, *The Right to Home School* (Durham, N.C.: Carolina Academic Press, 1998), 101.

16. *Care and Protection of Charles*, 504 N.E.2d 592 (Mass., 1987), in Christopher J. Klicka, *The Right to Home School* (Durham, N.C.: Carolina Academic Press, 1998), 44.

17. *New Jersey v. Massa*, 231 A. 2d 252 (1967).

18. *Wisconsin v. Yoder*, 406 U.S. 205 (1972), in Christopher J. Klicka, *The Right to Home School* (Durham, N.C.: Carolina Academic Press, 1998), 50.

19. Christopher J. Klicka, *The Right to Home School* (Durham, N.C.: Carolina Academic Press, 1998), 26.

Chapter 7: Caveat Emptor

1. Donald H. McLaughlin and Stephen Broughman, "Private Schools in the United States: A Statistical Profile, 1993–1994" (Washington, D.C.: American Institutes for Research, July 1997) ERIC, ED 409633, 9.

2. Newman, "Comparing Private Schools and Public Schools," 7.

3. Institute of Urban Life, Loyola University, Chicago, "Chicago's Private Elementary and Secondary Schools: Their Role in Neighborhood Revitalization" (report, 1998), 1.

4. "Welcome to ACSI on the Internet," <http://www.acsi.org/> (13 November 2001).

5. Tamara Henry and Anthony DeBarros, "Vouchers Enter Second Decade," *USA Today*, October 23, 2000, <http://www.edreform.com/news/001023usat.htm> (November, 2001).

6. Ibid.

7. Paul E. Peterson, William G. Howell, and Jay P. Greene, "An Evaluation of the Cleveland Voucher Program after Two Years" (paper prepared by the Program on Education Policy and Governance, Harvard University, June 1999), 1.

8. Henry and DeBarros, "Vouchers Enter Second Decade," 2.

9. "Voucher Wars" (editorial), *The Washington Post*.

10. Henry and DeBarros, "Vouchers Enter Second Decade," 4.

11. "School Vouchers: The Emerging Track Record" (a report of The National Education Association and The American Federation of Teachers, April 1999), <http://www.nea.org/issues/vouchers/voutrak_.html> (November 2001).

12. William G. Howell, Patrick J. Wolf, Paul E. Peterson, and David E. Campbell, "Test-Score Effects of School Vouchers in Dayton, Ohio, New York City, and Washington, D.C.: Evidence from Randomized Field Trials" (paper prepared for the annual meetings of the American Political Science Association, Washington, D.C., September 2000), 2.

13. McLaughlin and Broughman, *Private Schools in the United States*, 63.

14. Ibid.

15. Ibid.

16. Susan Black, "Less Is More," *The American School Board Journal* 186 (1999): 38.

17. Ibid., 39.

18. Jeremy D. Finn, "Class Size and Students at Risk" (1998), http://www.ed.gov/pubs/ClassSize/title.html> (13 November 2001).

19. Black, "Less Is More," 39.

20. Finn, "Class Size and Students at Risk."

21. Black, "Less is More," 40.

22. G. E. Robinson, "Synthesis of Research on Effects of Class Size," *Educational Leadership* 47 (1990): 80–90, in Jeremy D. Finn, "Class Size and Students at Risk" (1998), <http://www.ed.gov/pubs/ClassSize/title.html> (13 November 2001).

23. Steven Vryhof, "Why is Nels:88 Important?" *Christian Educators Journal* 32 (1992): 14–18.

24. S. Cates, "Teacher Perceived Problems in the Christian School" (unpublished manuscript, 1992), in Joe P. Sutton and Timothy G. Watson, "Barriers to Excellence: A National Survey of Teachers from the American Association of Christian Schools," *Journal of Research on Christian Education* 4 (1995): 23.

25. T. G. Watson (unpublished data, 1993 biannual survey of teacher education graduates), in Joe P. Sutton and Timothy G. Watson, "Barriers to Excellence: A National Survey of Teachers from the American Association of Christian Schools," *Journal of Research on Christian Education* 4 (1995): 24.

26. Joe P. Sutton and Timothy G. Watson, "Barriers to Excellence: A National Survey of Teachers from the American Association of Christian Schools," *Journal of Research on Christian Education* 4 (1995): 28.

27. John Van Dyk, "Can Christian Schools Change?" *Christian Educators Journal* 33 (1995): 5.

28. Bob Moore, "The Dangers of a Christian School Education," *Christian Educator's Journal* 37 (1997): 2.

29. Ibid., 2.

30. Guenter E. Salter, "The Problem with Christian Education: Ideational or Implementational Insufficiency?" *Balance*, newsletter, School of Education, Bob Jones University, vol. 9 (1988).

31. Ibid.

32. H. K. Zoeklicht, "A Beginning," *Christian Educators Journal* 31 (April 1992): 6.

Chapter 8: The Home Schooling Option

1. J. H. Selke, "Homeschooling Parental Stress and Social Support Scale: Initial Psychometric Evidence" (unpublished manuscript, University of California at Berkeley, 1996), 6.

2. Daniel Golden, "Homeschoolers Learn How to Gain Clout Inside the Beltway," *Wall Street Journal*, 24 April 2000.

3. Toby Harnden, "Dating to Be Banned at 'Home School' College," *The Daily (London) Telegraph*, 5 October 1999.

4. Lawrence M. Rudner, "Scholastic Achievement and Demographic Characteristics of Home School Students in 1998," *Education Policy Analysis Archives* (23 March 1999), <http://epaa.asu.edu/epaa/vyn8/> (November 2001).

5. Patricia Lines, *Home Instruction: The Size and Growth of the Movement*, in Jane Van Galen and Mary Anne Pitman, eds., *Home Schooling: Political,*

Historical, and Pedagogical Perspectives (New Jersey: Ablex Publishing Corporation, 1991), 36.

6. Cynthia Sulaiman, e-mail message to author, 14 June 2000.

7. Maralee Mayberry, "Teaching for the New Age: A Study of New Age Families Who Educate Their Children at Home," *Home School Researcher* 5 (1989): 12.

8. Valerie Lynn Witt, "A Descriptive Study and Needs Assessment of the Typical Washington Homeschool Family," *Home School Researcher* 13 (1999): 14.

9. Steven Gray, "Why Some Parents Choose to Home School," *Home School Researcher* 9 (1993): 5.

10. Jane A. Van Galen, "Ideologues and Pedagogues: Parents Who Teach Their Children at Home," in Jane Van Galen and Mary Anne Pitman, eds., *Home Schooling: Political, Historical, and Pedagogical Perspectives* (New Jersey: Ablex Publishing Corporation, 1991), 66.

11. Mary E. Hood, "Contemporary Philosophical Influences on the Home Schooling Movement," *Home School Researcher* 7 (1991): 6.

12. Steven Gray, "Why Some Parents Choose to Home School," 4.

13. J. F. Rakestraw, "Home Schooling in Alabama," *Home School Researcher* 4 (1988): 2.

14. J. Wartes, "Recent Results from the Washington Homeschool Research Project," *Home School Researcher* 6 (1990): 2.

15. H. B. Richman, W. Girten, and J. Snyder, "Academic Achievement and Its Relationship to Selected Variables Among Pennsylvania Homeschoolers," *Home School Researcher* 6 (1990): 10.

16. E. A. Frost, "A Descriptive Study of the Academic Achievement of Selected Elementary School-Aged Children Educated at Home in Five Illinois Counties" (Ed.D. diss., Northern Illinois University, 1987).

17. Rudner, "Home School Students in 1998," 19.

18. Michael Farris, *The Future of Home Schooling* (Washington, D.C.: Regnery Publishing, 1997), xii.

19. Ibid., xiii.

20. Paulo C. M. de Oliveira, Timothy G. Watson, and Joe P. Sutton, "Differences in Critical Thinking Skills Among Students Educated in Public Schools, Christian Schools, and Home Schools," *Home School Researcher* 10 (1994): 4.

21. Richard G. Medlin, "Creativity in Home Schooled Children," *Home School Researcher* 12 (1996): 10.

22. Steven D. Smith, Jilanne Bannink-Misiewicz, and Shelly Bareman, "A Comparison of the Fundamental Motor Skill Abilities of Home School and Conventional School Children," *Home School Researcher* 8 (1992): 4.

23. Dale DeVoe, Cathy Kennedy, and Crystal A. Lloyd, "Physical Fitness and Activity Characteristics of Home Schooled Children," *Home School Researcher* 12 (1996): 6.

24. J. W. Taylor, "Self-Concept in Home Schooling Children," *Home School Researcher* 2 (1986): 1.

25. S. W. Kelley, "Socialization of Home Schooled Children: A Self-Concept Study," *Home School Researcher* 7 (1991): 5.

26. Paul Kitchen, "Socialization of Home School Children Versus Conventional School Children," *Home School Researcher* 7 (1991): 10.

27. L. E. Shyers, "A Comparison of Social Adjustment between Home and Traditionally Schooled Students" (Ph.D. diss., University of Florida, 1992).

28. Witt, "A Descriptive Study and Needs Assessment," 9.

29. Vicki D. Tillman, "Home Schoolers, Self-Esteem, and Socialization," *Home School Researcher* 11 (1995): 5.

30. Thomas C. Smedley, "Socialization of Home School Children," *Home School Researcher* 8 (1992): 14.

31. Tillman, "Home Schoolers, Self-Esteem, and Socialization," 4.

32. Richard G. Medlin, "Homeschooling and the Question of Socialization," *Peabody Journal of Education* 75 (1 & 2), 112.

33. Theodore E. Wade, *The Home School Manual* (Auburn, California: Gazelle Publications, 1984): 35.

34. Gray, "Why Some Parents Choose to Home School," 6.

35. Richard G. Medlin, "Home Schooling: What's Hard? What Helps?" *Home School Researcher* 11 (1996): 4.

36. Mark A. Resetar, "An Exploratory Study of the Rationales Parents Have for Home Schooling," *Home School Researcher* 6 (1990): 5.

37. James W. Boothe, Leo H. Bradley, Michael T. Flick, and Susanne P. Kirk, "No Place Like Home," *The American School Board Journal* 184 (1997): 39.

38. Witt, "A Descriptive Study and Needs Assessment," 12.

Chapter 9: Dodging the Silver-Bullet Mentality

1. Mortimer B. Zuckerman, "The Times of Our Lives," *U.S. News and World Report*, 27 December 1999, 69.

2. Susan Green, e-mail message to author, 18 April 2000.

3. "Profile of the Class of 2004" (table), *Facts: The Stanford Undergraduate Program*, <http://www.stanford.edu/home/stanford/facts/undergraduate.html#profile> (9 November 2001).

4. *High School Preparation: Questions*, under the question "Does it matter whether an applicant attends a public or private secondary school?" <http://web.mit.edu/Admissions/www/undergrad/freshman/faq/hsprep.html> (9 November 2001).

5. Jodie Morse, "Is That Your Final Answer?" *Time*, 19 June 2000, 34.

6. William Bennett, "A Nation Still at Risk," *Policy Review* 90 (1998): 28.

7. Ruth Ann Wells, e-mail message to author, 27 January 2000.

8. U.S. Department of Education Charter Schools, "Overview of Charter Schools," <http://www.uscharterschools.org/pub/uscs_dcs/gi/overview.htm> (November 2001).

9. Thomas L. Good and Jennifer S. Braden, "Charter Schools: Another Reform Failure or a Worthwhile Investment?" *Phi Delta Kappan* 81 (June 2000): 746.

10. Lowell C. Rose and Alec M. Gallup, "The 32nd Annual Phi Delta Kappa/Gallup Poll of the Public's Attitudes toward the Public Schools," *Phi Delta Kappan* 82 (September 2000), <http://www.pdkintl.org/kappan/kpol0009.htm> (November 2001).

11. U.S. Department of Education Charter Schools, "Overview of Charter Schools."

12. U.S. Department of Education Charter Schools, "Arizona Charter School Information," <http://www.uscharterschools.org/pub/sp/2> (November 2001).

13. U.S. Department of Education Charter Schools, "Enrollment by State," <http://www.ed.gov/pubs/charter4thyear/b.html> (November 2001).

14. "Back-to-School Bulletin #3" (Washington, D.C.: The Center for Education Reform, 2001), <http://www.edreform.com/press/2001/010917.html> (November 2001).

15. U.S. Department of Education Charter Schools, "Arkansas Charter School Information," <http://www.uscharterschools.org/pub/sp/28> (November 2001).

16. Dave Weber, "Charter Schools Fall Short," *Orlando Sentinel*, 18 May 2001.

17. Ibid.

18. "New Data Makes Case for Charter Schools" (Washington, D.C.: The Center for Education Reform, 2001), <http://www.edreform.com/press/2001/newdata.htm> (November 2001).

19. Ibid.

20. "The Not-So-Ugly Duckling," *The Wall Street Journal*, 4 May 2001, in The Center for Education Reform, Washington, D.C., 2001, <http://www.edreform.com/news/2001/010504wsj.htm> (November 2001).

21. Ibid.

22. The Center for Education Reform, Washington, D.C., 2001, "Survey of Charter Schools, 2000–2001 Introduction," <http://www.edreform.com/charter_schools/report/survey01.html> (November 2001).

23. Jeanne Allen, "Education by Charter: The New Neighborhood Schools" (Washingtion, D.C.: The Center for Education Reform, 2001), <http://www.edreform.com/pubs/ncpa.htm> (November 2001).

24. Ibid.

25. Donald Waldrip, "A Brief History and Philosophy of Magnet Schools" (2001) <http://www.magnet.edu/history.html> (November 2001).

26. Morton Inger, "Improving Urban Education with Magnet Schools," ERIC Clearinghouse on Urban Education, ERIC, ED 340813, <http://www.ed.gov/databases/ERIC_Digests/ed340813.html> (November 2001).

27. Ibid.

28. Ibid.

29. Ibid.

30. Ibid.

31. Robert L. Simonds, *A Guide to the Public Schools* (Costa Mesa, California: ACE/CEE, 1993), 5.

32. Research Services, Peoria Public Schools, Peoria, Illinois, faxed message to author, 3 June 2000.

33. Department of English Language Acquisition, Denver Public Schools, Denver, Colorado, e-mail message to author, 20 June 2000.

34. Orange County Public Schools, Orlando, Florida, faxed message to author, 22 June 2000.

35. Donna Joy Boxerman, e-mail message to author, 2 February 2000.

36. Ruth Ann Wells, e-mail message to author, 27 January 2000.

37. Chiara R. Nappi, "Local Illusions," *The Wilson Quarterly* 23 (1999): 46.

38. *Learn in Freedom*, "Nobel Prize Winners Hate School," <http://learn-infreedom.org/Nobel_hates_school.html> (13 November 2001).

39. Josh Tyrangiel, "How Do You Spell Smarty-Pants?" *Time*, 12 June 2000, 99.

40. Ruth Ann Wells, e-mail message to author, 27 January 2000.